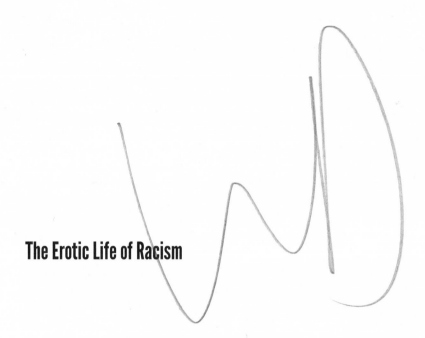

The Erotic Life of Racism

The Erotic Life
of Racism

Sharon Patricia Holland

DURHAM AND LONDON 2012

DUKE UNIVERSITY PRESS

© 2012 Duke University Press
All rights reserved
Printed in the United States of
America on acid-free paper ∞
Designed by Kristina Kachele
Typeset in Minion by Keystone
Typesetting, Inc.
Library of Congress Cataloging-in-
Publication Data appear on the
last printed page of this book.

You can't be what you were
So you better start being
just what you are
—Fugazi, "Bad Mouth"

Contents

Acknowledgments

The Erotic Life of Racism has had several permutations over the last decade.
It first started as a book about "generations"—a book that, thankfully, Ken
Wissoker at Duke University Press suggested I didn't want to write. It then
became a more conventional project by taking on the shape of an introduction, a few chapters demonstrating my theoretical rubric, and a tidy conclusion. That manuscript made it through the first round of reviews, but it
wasn't yet a book—it hadn't yet become the project I wanted to write. I
thank the readers on that second attempt for suffering through a fledgling
project. In the two years after that second attempt, I began to write a rather
long introduction to the existing project—one that comprised some fifty
pages or more of analysis. I took this portion of the project to a writing
group with Cathy Davidson—it was there that she suggested I siphon off
the expository chapters of the book and concentrate on the theoretical

side. In that moment, *The Erotic Life of Racism* began to blossom and take its present shape.

The title came before the book itself, calling me to write a book that could measure up in some way to the weight of that phrase. I do not know if I have succeeded in this task. Over the last decade that this project took shape, there have been many people and institutions to which I am indebted. I hope in my brief recounting that I do not forget anyone along the way.

I would first like to thank the University of Illinois, Chicago; Northwestern University; and Duke University for providing generous research funds to support this project, and for providing, perhaps unwittingly, the institutional experiences that continued to demonstrate to me that there was a need for it. During a crucial phase in the development of the book, I received a Senior Lectureship in American Studies from the Fulbright Foundation. While teaching two courses at Universidad Complutense ("La Complu"), I was able to present work that would eventually become part of this book. In particular I would like to thank Isabel Duran Gimenez-Rico, Carmen Mendez García, and Ana Antón-Pacheco Bravo, my wonderful colleagues at the university. I also extend a heartfelt thank you to the graduate students in my feminist theory course—their responses to the articles and books we read were often unpredictable and thoroughly stimulating. Thank you for a wonderful five months in Madrid.

This book would not have been possible without my colleagues in feminist studies, queer studies, and critical race theory. Their work has inspired me to write this little treatise as homage to the brilliance and the fine critique found in the interstices. May they see vestiges of their words throughout these pages, as this one is, I hope, for all of us. I would like to thank Jennifer Brody for pulling the beginnings of this project out of the trash, putting the pieces back together, and setting them on my desk late one night along with some simple words to greet me with my morning coffee: "Keep writing this."

Thanks to Darcy, who always came through, and to Jacob Mueller whose passion for interdisciplinarity is infectious and whose presence in the classroom I will always miss. To Michael Main, who is among the best of graduate studies assistants and who kept my calendar open for work on this project and often reminded me of where I needed to be and how I should get there. I still miss you. To my dear friend Chris Messenger, who knows all things Faulkner and whose teaching is impeccable. Thanks also to the graduate students in the University of Illinois, Chicago, seminar that Chris and I taught together. Our readings and discussions in that classroom led to some of the questions that became the conclusion for this project. Thanks to Janet Messenger, whose diversity of talents is an inspiration. Thanks also to the graduate students in my Critical Race Theory seminar at Northwestern—they are a fierce group of folks with intellectual acumen and compassion. The seminar was a banner one and I thank you all. To Wannalee Romero whose wit, grace, and serious rigor pushed my research along at a crucial moment—thanks for keeping it all together while I was in Madrid. To Robin, Nicole, and Folayemi whose voices in my undergraduate seminar on feminist literature still ring, and whose visits to my office hours were always delightful and a welcome break from the e-mails and committee responsibilities. To Anna Kivlan, who worked tirelessly on copyediting and checking notes for accuracy, often filling in missing information and providing crucial last-minute library searches for materials.

Toward the end of the project I made my first return trip to Chicago, where I had spent the better part of the last decade. I thank Greg Laski, Wannalee Romero, and Melissa Daniels for welcoming me back with open arms—I will always remember that homecoming evening. To my Chicago family, words cannot express how much I miss you and hold you in my heart always. Lisa Freeman and Heather Schmucker, thanks for being my homegirls and for holding me when I need it most. Jennifer Brier and Kat Hindmand, I miss your warmth and love. I give thanks to Judith Sensibar for her help with the Faulkner section and for her encouragement, and I thank David Sensibar for his love of wine and support of all of my endeavors. Thanks also to Judy Raphael and Tony Philips whose creative vision has touched me in more ways than I can count. To E. Patrick Johnson and Stephen Lewis, I remember you both every time I sit down to a beautiful meal. To Mark Canuel, for his friendship and Capricorn love. To Johari Jobir, your intellectual companionship is sorely missed—Ralph Lauren is holding a table for us.

Toward the end of writing this book, I purchased eight acres and moved into the woods at the back of a watershed. I did not know it at the time, but the land I now call "home" was once part of one of the largest black farmsteads in North Carolina. A friend suggested that I call it "Sweet Negritude"—the land here signals all the permutations of the life, love, and mystery of blackness. I give thanks to all of my friends in North Carolina who have kept me going through three very difficult years—Kim Turk, Cate Smith, and Bruce, Doreen, Josie, and Katie Sanfelici. To Christine Callan at Copa Vida and Tracy Gill at Joe Van Gogh, thanks for keeping the coffee going while I wrote, revised, and wrote again. To Laurabelle and the gang at Watts for keeping me fed and letting me laugh out loud. To Kathy Rudy whose love of animals matches my own, and to Kristine Stiles whose friendship is steady and enduring. To Shelba and Starr, bright lights in the Carolina sky. To all the horses, hounds, and humans at Terrell's Creek— thanks for welcoming me and helping me enjoy the ride. With the animals on my mind: to Samar and Ebenezer, who I long for every day, and to Winnie and Webster, who run away but always come back home. I also would like to thank Ken Wissoker and Jade Brooks at Duke University Press for their faith in this project, and of course, thanks to my meticulous readers whose generosity of engagement was more than any author could expect or ask for.

The last group of thanks goes to my family, near and far. To Yoshi Campbell—your love for me is unwavering and I am proud to call you "sister." To my homegirls Sylvia Villarreal and Tae Hart who know me. To Tom, Ella, and Muriel Beyer—see you at the Cape again for another jelly- fish rights symposium. To Meta Dewa Jones and family—steady, wise, and always there for me. To Ryan and Liz Ananat—I am proud in so many ways, not least among them to be the "grandmother" of your little one. To Anne Cubilie, who knows how to cut through bullshit like a knife through butter—thanks for taking me through the fire. To Etan Nasreddin-Longo who sees all things and just knows. To Kathleen J. McCabe—a writer's writer and whose advice, friendship, and careful eye helped to bring this project home. Thanks to my mother for being the fiercest protector of my righteous mind. And finally to the Holland clan (Lexus, Flip, and Jackie)— we take a licking and keep on ticking—but especially to Jackie, whose big heart is something to aspire to.

Dismayingly, institutionalized racism and prejudice endure too, long after the abolition of slavery, or the desegregation of public institutions, or the protest marches or the shattering acts of violence. Racism, it turns out, can take the heat.
—Joy Gregory, on her adaptation of Studs Terkel's "Race: How Blacks and Whites Think and Feel about the American Obsession"

Most horrific acts committed by one person against another occur as small thoughtless gestures under mundane, if not trite, circumstances.
—Jennifer Culbert, "Beyond Intention"

The erotic is the mode of subjective communication.
—Deborah Bergoffen, "Out from Under"

It is time to recognize the political dimensions of erotic life.
—Gayle Rubin, "Thinking Sex"

Introduction

The Last Word on Racism

A few days after Tupac Shakur's death in 1996, I pulled into a Safeway parking lot in Palo Alto, California, with my friend's fifteen-year-old daughter, Danielle. We were listening to one of Shakur's songs on the radio; because he was a hometown boy, the stations were playing his music around the clock—a kind of electromagnetic vigil, if you will. An older (but not elderly) woman with a grocery cart came to the driver's side of my car and asked me to move my vehicle so that she could unload her groceries. The tone of her voice assumed fruition—it was not only a request but a demand that would surely be met. The Southerner in me would have been happy to help; the critic in me didn't understand why she simply couldn't put her groceries in on the other side where there were no other cars or potential impediments. I told the woman that I would gladly wait in my car until she unloaded her groceries—that way, there would be plenty of room for her to maneuver.

While she did this, I continued to listen to Shakur's music and talk with Danielle. We were "bonding," and I was glad that she was talking to me about how Shakur's death was affecting her and her classmates. When I noticed that the woman had completed her unloading, I got out and we walked behind her car toward the Safeway. What happened next has stayed with me as one of the defining moments of my life in Northern California. As we passed the right rear bumper of her car, she said with mustered indignation, "And to think I marched for you!" I was stunned at first—when something like this happens to you, you see the whole event in slow motion. I recovered and decided that I had two options: to walk away without a word or to confront the accusation—to model for Danielle how to handle with a modicum of grace what would surely be part of the fabric of her life as a black woman in the United States. I turned to the woman and said, "You didn't march for me, you marched for yourself—and if you don't know that, I can't help you."

When average people participate in racist acts, they demonstrate a profound misreading of the subjects they encounter. The scene related above dramatizes a host of racialized relations: the expectation that black women will cease a connection with their own families in order to respond to the needs of white persons; the comprehension of a refusal to do so as a criminal act; the need to subject black bodies to the rule of race; and the absolute denial of the connection between seemingly disparate peoples that the phrase "civil rights march" connotes. For that woman in the parking lot, the civil rights struggle was not about freedom for us all, it was about acquiring a kind of purchase on black life. I would be given the right to participate in "democratic process," but the ability to exercise the autonomy inherent in such a right would be looked upon with disdain and, at times, outrage.

The scene from the parking lot stays with me as if the woman and I were locked in a past that has tremendous purchase on my present. In my mind, we hover there touching one another with the lie of difference and nonrelation balancing precariously between us—like the characters Rosa and Clytie at war on the dilapidated staircase in William Faulkner's *Absalom, Absalom!*, a scene I explicate at some length in the conclusion of this book. The psychic violation of that moment in the parking lot haunts me still;

but it is the intimacy of that moment that arrests me. *That woman expected something from me*—one usually does not expect anything from strangers. Moreover, our connection as women, tenuous though it might have been, was completely obscured, if not obliterated, by this racist act. It was then that I began to think about "race" under the auspices of racism, the thing that according to the epigraph for this chapter "endures."

Racism defends us against the project of universal belonging, against the findings, if you will, of the human genome project. Racism, after all, "can take the heat." Perhaps racism can take the heat because of its "universal" appeal. One of the first tenets of critical race theory is that "racism is ordinary."[1] For scholars of critical race theory, "racism" is almost always articulated as an everyday occurrence, as pedestrian rather than spectacular, although we have seen evidence of its *gendered* spectacularity through historical watersheds such as Emmett Till (both then and now) and James Byrd.[2]

In this project my first grounding is in the work of critical race theory, with the understanding that *everyday* racism defines race, interprets it, and decrees what the personal and institutional work of race will be. My second grounding is in the work of sexuality studies and queer theory; both are critical projects dedicated to various articulations of the erotic lives of individuals. In this book I will demonstrate that although contemporary sexuality studies and queer theory have committed themselves to a thoroughgoing analysis of racist practice, rarely do they actually succeed in this endeavor. Can work on "desire" be antiracist work? Can antiracist work *think* "desire"? What would happen if we opened up the erotic to a scene of racist hailing? In this work I attempt to enrich conversations about our erotic life and our racist practice. I contend that it is possible to have both conversations at the same time, and in the same space of such intimate subjugation.

Racism requires one to participate in what I would call a *project of belonging* if the work of producing racial difference(s) is to reach fruition. I have used the phrase "project of belonging" to signify two sets of relations. One is a "real," biological connection, a belonging that occurs at the level of family (blood relation). A crude understanding of race is that it is always already the thing that happens in the blood: think "one-drop rule," "blood quantum," "blueblood," or "sangre pura." The second set of relations is the result of the work of identifying with others, a belonging usually imposed by a community *or* by one's own choice. Given the slipperiness of identity, identifying with others can be a fictitious and fantastic undertaking. Fantasy, of course, can oscillate between delusion and creative hope. As Robert Miles and Malcolm Brown observe, "In the everyday world, the facts of biological difference are secondary to the meanings that are attributed to them."[3] Here it is meaning that matters. In the purely existential accounting, human beings make meaning everyday and we have come to understand, like Miles and Brown, that such matter(s) *creates* the materiality of race. My work in *The Erotic Life of Racism* interrogates the meaning of such creative ambitions and argues that we don't create meaning as much as we reproduce it.

Joy Gregory's words given in the first epigraph ground racism in what appears to be the long history of black suffering in the United States. In short, desegregation, abolition, and protest marches conjure black bodies so very readily; it is almost as if we think of those events as belonging to "the black experience"—and in many ways they do. What I want to open up here is the possibility that these events might not only signal black physical and political forms, but also mark a profound revision of the place we have come to know and call home. What if these histories no longer belonged to a people but instead comprised what we mean when we say the word "American"? I want to argue that when we see and say "race," regardless of how much we intend to understand race as being had by everyone, our examples of racial being and racist targets are often grounded in *black matter(s)*. In this instance, the black body is the quintessential sign for subjection, for a particular experience that it must inhabit and own *all by itself.*

What better way to think about how this conjuring of the black body works than through the anecdote with which I begin this book. I use this incident not to make a point about its universality and thus elevate it to privileged status (although I know that at some point this might be unavoidable), but rather to elicit both the intimacy and the quotidian nature of racism. A scene of everyday racist practice opens in two directions: one in which the scene focuses relentlessly upon the individual, seemingly to the exclusion of such leitmotifs of antiracist struggle as structure and caste; and the other in which the event unravels a series of dependencies and intimacies both unexplored and unexplained. It is this latter direction that I hope the reader will both follow and find intriguing. In the final analysis quotidian racism can seem rather *unremarkable*; my point is to bring what cannot be remarked upon without some embarrassment to fuller recognition and accounting. To this end, that woman in the parking lot wanted a connection with me—one solidified through time and place by a history, a genealogy that she could readily attach to me. In short, she hailed me, and rather than respond in kind, *I spoke*. To make matters worse, my tiny little speech act in a Safeway parking lot became a contentless utterance—which was confirmed by her look of surprise, if not horror, when I opened my mouth. Her pronouncement was not designed to elicit a response, it was fashioned to keep me in my place. My retort offered her an alternative model—a refraction rather than a reflection of her own situatedness. As Toni Morrison once reminded us, "Definitions belong to the definers not the defined."[4] Clearly.

Where racism imposes racial purity, however, *law and practice* will code identification across differences as impossible—even if it happens, even if it is real.[5] Even though every human visage and quotidian encounter bears witness to miscegenation's imprint, miscegenation remains an impossibility; we are still made to choose a category, to state who our people are, and to relate to one cultural mode of being over and against another as if categories, communities, and belonging are positioned in finite relationship. As Adrian Piper notes in her essay "Passing for White, Passing for Black": "In this country, . . . the fact of African ancestry among whites ranks up there with family incest, murder, and suicide as one of the bitterest and most difficult pills for white Americans to swallow."[6] It is interesting that Piper counts incest as one of the holy trinity of family travesties; as scholars of Southern history and literature in particular have indicated, incest is frequently miscegenation in the Southern imaginary. In other words, because of chattel slavery we cannot readily separate the practice of incest and the occurrence of miscegenation. We can't have one without the other, yet we are so confused about the matter of race—who has it, how did we get it, is it just "culture" after all—that we have managed to spin exciting yarns about its place in our "family" histories.[7] For example, more than twenty years ago I discovered that my father's father was in fact a "white" man, and it took me another decade to call him "grandfather" with any real conviction.

I use the phrase "blood strangers" to articulate this cognitive dissonance in order to mine the contradiction between human practice and collective (mis)understanding.[8] While race creates the possibility for blood strangers, it also employs its primary ally and enforcer, "racism," to police the imaginary boundary between blood (us) and strangers (them). Racism transforms an already porous periphery into an absolute, thereby making it necessary to deny all kinds of crossings. Moreover, even when those crossings appear less obvious—when women appear together in a quotidian scene of racist violence, for example—racism succeeds in breaking the tacit connection between them. In other words, racism irrevocably changes gendered relationships. Racism can also be described as the emotional lifeblood of race; it is the "feeling" that articulates and keeps the flawed logic of race in its place. When assessment is on the line, the "races" take their seats at the American feast of difference. This is the catch-22 of race: it renders theorizing about "it" impossible because it stabilizes identity for those who *impose* it and for those who work to *expose* it.

In this book I seek to mine the interstice between the insistence of critical race theory upon the "ordinary" in racist practice and the call by queer theory for us to take care of the *feeling* that escapes or releases when bodies collide in pleasure and in pain. This interstice is the moment—the blip in time—that is of great importance to my work here.[9] We focus on race, but rarely on the *everyday* system of terror and pleasure that in varying proportions makes race so useful a category of difference. But siting and citing everyday racism is almost like stating a belief in the paranormal. Racism dismembers the "real"—so robs and eviscerates it that nothing and no one can appear as "whole" in its strange and brutal refraction.

One of the chief arguments of my project is that race coheres in the everyday practice of familial belonging. Since "the family" has not only been the cornerstone of liberal ideology but also black community belonging, it is important to ask—nearly 150 years after the abolition of slavery—whether or not the preservation of the idea of the "black" family is working for us.[10] This is not a query that can be politely asked or answered but it is a necessary one, and this project seeks to begin not by rehashing the race/culture debate but simply by asking if the same scaffolding that applies to *quotidian* racist practice might not also be the same structure that engenders the survival of the core concept of blackness, especially as such a concept relates to notions of familial and community belonging. The turn toward the quotidian is not one that focuses on prejudice but rather on the discretionary acts and, yes, racist practices that each of us make in everyday decisions such as choosing someone to sit beside on the subway, selecting a mate or a sperm donor, or developing a list of subjects for an academic study. The autonomy usually attached to erotic choices should be reevaluated to think through these attachments.

In order to worry that every day, to think about how much racism demands of us, from us, this book returns to that somewhat banal pairing otherwise known as the black/white binary. Such a return, to echo Hortense Spillers, might be "embarrassing" or "backward."[11] When race becomes the basis for social organization—determining and fixing not only what we are to others, but also defining who we are—it gains an immutability that neither pro nor con can shake—it gains ontological might and becomes "too high to get over, too low to get under."[12]

This book moves in the direction of prevailing work in critical race theory—toward racism and away from race—with one, if not two, caveats. It is my contention that we cannot get away from the black/white binary while thinking through the work of racism. In calls to abandon the black/white dichotomy for more expansive readings of racism's spectacular effects, critics often ignore the psychic life of racism. What appears as an opening up or an expansion of the territory from "race and racism" to "racisms" might simply be a misrecognition of the primary work of racism.[13] In the beginning moments of *Against Race*, Paul Gilroy offers the reflection that "black and white are bonded together by the mechanism of 'race' that estrange them from each other and amputate their common humanity."[14] Gilroy's visceral insight is a testament to the fact that we cannot get away from our interpretation of the primary work of race at the junction of black and white; the estrangement that Gilroy alludes to is odd, given that relations between the two are and have been so intimately articulated.[15]

While I do not want to contest that globalization indeed has resulted in a proliferation of "racisms," I do want to insist stubbornly that the psychic life of racism can best be read in the context of the United States in the space where black and white intersect, where the outer limit of doing and being are exercised and felt by those who seek to negotiate their place at the "American" table. I say this even as someone who has great investments in the fields of Afro-Native and Native American studies. What I am driving at here is simple: even though critics want to move away from a black/ white binary toward a more "open" field of inquiry, the way in which we understand how racism manifests itself is through a black/white example that belies a very static, but necessary, repetitious reading of racist practice. What work, critical or otherwise, have we performed to move beyond an interaction that to begin with we barely have been able to be truthful about (to ourselves, to others)? If anything, the chatter on the left and on the right during the presidential campaign of Barack Obama in 2008 assures us that we are by no means ready to give up the binary.[16] It performs a fantastic service for us.

In this book I seek to correct a consistent *misreading of racist practice.* Too often the insidiousness of slavery casts a long shadow over the inter- pretive work that we perform; in our effort to uncover a terrible wrong, "a woeful shame," "a national embarrassment," we sometimes want to read the present as if it actually lived in this same dreadful past. We exist in a kind of Nietzschean ethics—where the present is consistently the past's particular factotum.[17] In this drama the parts are cast and we play them to their fullest, and because these relations have been cemented it is difficult for us to see beyond them to something else that might motivate us. This familiar reiteration in black and white has an equal and opposite upshot: it prevents "slavery" (writ large) from being seen in all of its formative mach- inations. Instead, slavery is relegated to its black and white players in a past, which desperately needs to be forgotten. I am not sure if that something else alluded to above exists or is even worth our contemplation, because to move forward in this moment, given all that has happened, would surely be like committing suicide—of a generational sort. But, at the risk of being contrary, this project goes to that territory.

The theoretical exploration I make here encourages us to reimagine the connection between black and white and to open up the interstitial and charged space between critical race theory and queer theory. This text and its readings therefore serve as an arrest in a seemingly perpetual critical backward motion. In queering the inquiry, for example—in returning to the black/white binary and asking what really happens or happened there

—we might be able to consider, at least for a moment, what our "pleasure" might look like; what being together, figuratively and literally, might yield —aside from, at times, the miscegenated being.[18] As I mentioned earlier, I am also aware that such a focus on the black/white binary in terms of queer studies might seem backward in and of itself. As Tavia Nyong'o points out, "theory . . . can present itself as being explicitly 'about' race, class, and sexuality while continuing to serve the function of regulation and discipline. A major aspect of this regulation . . . is the frozen dialectic between black and white, and . . . between straight and queer, that is produced and reproduced within cultural forms both sophisticated and otherwise."[19] In this book I want to *defrost* that signal dialectic—to revise the black/white encounter's oppositional narrative to speak to us across place and (in)appropriate time.

So often our "racist" culture is held as separate and apart from our desiring selves. To think about desire is to arrive at a queer place. But I do not mean for that queer place to become overdetermined by its association with desire, with the erotic. In essence, I am opening the door to a notion of the "erotic" that oversteps the category of the autonomous so valued in queer theory so as to place the erotic—the personal and political dimension of desire—at the threshold of ideas about quotidian racist practice. As Simone de Beauvoir reminds us in *The Second Sex*: "The erotic experience is one that most poignantly reveals to human beings their ambiguous condition."[20] It is this striking ambiguity that not only brings us back to the quotidian but also to the strange and often violent modes of racist practice.[21] I use the erotic also to capture some sense of its historical connection to feminist phenomenological thought, a process that I outline in chapter 2 of this book.

When I invoke the phrase "queer place," I am thinking of queers here in much the same way as Randall Halle understands this constituency: "Not the acts in which they engage but rather the coercive norms that place their desires into a position of conflict with the present order."[22] My project comes from the other end of that question; rather than see desire as the force that "conflict[s] with the present order," I enlist the erotic as a possible harbinger *of the established order*. In doing so, I want to imagine what happens to the "white" side of the equation—what happens to whiteness in close proximity to blackness—and what happens to our conceptualization of the "us"? At the outset, it is important to note that I do not attempt, in the words of Michael Hames-García, to "recast questions of race into the language of desire."[23] Rather, by thinking about racism as quotidian practice, much like the critical race theorists whom I deeply admire, I understand racism as wielding incredible power in its ordering of *family*, *generation*, and *desire*—in both black and white.

The focus on moving "beyond" race and its black/white binary—a condition I myself have wished for and often depended upon—actually speaks to a persistent problem inherent in the black/white encounter: namely, that this crossing seems impossible; that this crossing almost never happens. In other words, what happens when someone who exists in time meets someone who only occupies space?[24] Those who order the world, who are world-making master time—those animals *and* humans who are perceived as having no world-making effects—merely occupy space. When James Baldwin asked, "How much *time* do you want for your progress?" he was marking this dichotomy.[25] If the black appears as the antithesis of history (occupies space), the white represents the industry of progressiveness (being in time). It is possible to surmise that resistance to this binary might actually be telling a truth about our sense of time and space instead of a truth about the meeting itself. We often talk of inequalities that emerge in black/white meeting, but we rarely understand those structural impediments and inequalities in terms of the phenomenological readings of time and space. For example, to return to my opening narrative, in that moment in the parking lot I was occupying space; the woman was not only occupying time but also performing her ability to represent its material nature. My temporal immateriality yoked my presence to the needs and desires of my white female counterpart; my inability to serve therefore represented an intrusion upon the woman's daily activities. I became an affront to *the order of things*, and her comment "to think I marched for you" was an invitation to take my place among the officially sanctioned table of contents for black/white herstory and relation.

At points in this project I return to the problem of "history" with varying degrees of critical success. In theoretical discourse, generally speaking, we have been bound by a fervent desire to make sure that we are historically grounded. In queer theory especially, this historical arc has been fleshed out through the work of Michel Foucault.[26] While Foucault's historical trajectory for the invention of the homosexual in the mid-nineteenth century is pathbreaking, it glides over signal events in the Americas such as transatlantic slavery or Indian removal as if these events bear no mark upon our sexual proclivities. In this mode of inquiry, a whole array of fruitful belongings, imaginings, and gestures can go unremarked upon and ultimately undervalued in critical discourse about sexuality. When the problem of history is laid at our feet, the imagined place for the black body is (re)produced out of the thin air at the critical heights of queer theory. This thin air mires the "black" in absolute relationship to the "white" as if their belonging were carved in glacial ice. The air up there is frosty indeed, and to speak about the black body at that atmospheric level is to produce a narrative of degradation to which that body is perpetually mired.

My argument with history, therefore, is not about its necessary efficacy or its archival rigor; my contention here is with how it is used to either fix a critical trajectory for a discipline (in the case of queer theory especially) or to ground a discussion of race in appropriate histories of black and white peoples in particular. In attempting to wade through the materials in the fruitful critical and fictive exchanges that I highlight, I find that history has a very limited reach where black/white bodies are concerned. As I have stated earlier, even though integration is our gold standard, we seem wholly unable to practice it *critically*.

I begin this book with a scene in a Safeway parking lot, and I end it with a reading of one of the central chapters of Faulkner's *Absalom, Absalom!* The material in between is mostly taken from critical theory, and given the stakes of my project—in queerness, blackness, and gender—Faulkner's signature and very canonical work might seem like an odd capstone. Faulkner's novel is a searing and relentless catalogue of racism's battle for the American soul. As he observes at one point in Miss Rosa Coldfield's narrative: "There is something in the touch of flesh with flesh which abrogates, cuts sharp and straight across the devious intricate channels of decorous ordering, which enemies as well as lovers know because it makes them both."[27] Abrogate. Enemies. Lovers. These words help to mark the complicated trajectory of racist practice, and to me it felt perfect to end this book with one of the most articulate manifestos about how to begin the process of repudiating such abrogation.

At the same time, my choice of *Absalom, Absalom!* resists the urge to find

what I term the "black.female.queer" representation as the obvious repository if not endpoint for a project that as it evolves seeks to find how we
lost this representation in the first place. The goal here is to get comfortable with that loss so that we can account for our forgetting in the
first instant while simultaneously marking such a moment by *not* replacing
the representation, by not making the obvious critical move to recover
black.female.queer with an appropriate sign of her belonging. The periods
in my configuration are meant to place the terms in figurative contestation,
reflecting both the ease with which such terms are grouped and the relative
incommensurability of the terms in critical conversation.

It is my hope that as scholars move through this book they might begin
to uncouple their own critical trajectories, if not desires, from their usual
embeddedness. My hope, further, is that there might be new spaces opened
up for finding what we have lost or forgotten without the customary urge
to reestablish the object of our desire, so to speak. In that space of the
erotic—the political and the personal—we might be able (if not ready) to
revise or even resist the object(s) of our critical desire as we come to
understand just what it takes to make the erotic such a generative space. I
am interested in outlining one aspect of the critical condition rather than
displaying a repertoire of somewhat prescriptive endings to a story that is
still unfolding.

I open chapter 1 with a sampling of pertinent critical race theory arguments about race and racism as a way to explore how such arguments have
helped to diversify the critical field of antiracist study. In this chapter I
perform what I hope is an important intervention by reading across a
spectrum of critical race theory work, thus demonstrating that there is
much to be gleaned from concerted attention to the field's many critical
corridors and interdisciplinary claims. In chapter 2, I stage the interface
between "the erotic" and "racist practice" by delving into the relationship
between feminist theories of the erotic from the mid to late twentieth century and how these theories have paved the way for the erotic's *disarticula-
tion* from racist practice. I argue that the erotic gains its autonomy during
the feminist sexuality debates in the early 1980s and that such erotic autonomy becomes central to the articulation of a queer studies project, much to
the detriment of a critical antiracist practice. In chapter 3, I return to the
kind of inquiry evidenced in the first chapter, as I read across a range of

queer studies work that positions itself in response to an overwhelmingly (white) queer theory. Given what the black/white binary tells us (or does not) about racist practice, I argue that the continual staging of one (racial) project over and against the other serves to harness black.female.queer (a constellation that I use throughout that chapter) in static relation to queer studies as a whole, such that this body (of work) is literally lost as an active critical voice. Finally, in the conclusion I perform a reading of Jacques Derrida's "The Last Word on Racism" / "Racism's Last Word" and his theory about "touch" in the context of one of the most important black/white interactions in American literature—the meeting of Rosa Coldfield and Clytie Sutpen on the staircase during the only chapter narrated by Miss Rosa in Faulkner's *Absalom, Absalom!*

In speaking to my classes on critical race and sexuality theory over the years, it has become clear to me that our methodology for thinking through the queer body can be cited along three registers: the psychoanalytic, the critique of global capital, and the biopolitical.[28] This project will move through a range of work dedicated to these epistemological registers but will resist the temptation to be seduced by one method of inquiry over another. My attempt here is to redirect our theoretical underpinnings, and my implicit question is whether or not these discourses are aiding us in our attention to the specter of racist practice that intermittently haunts queer studies conferences.[29] In many ways the responsibility for "fixing" the problem of race in academic discourse seems to have landed in our queer laps. But why? What is the underexplored connection between sexuality and race that makes us believe we can solve for x when other disciplinary endeavors have seemed unable to do so or have abandoned the project altogether? What can queer theory's desire do for understanding racist practice? Perhaps there is an answer to this question in the early work of Hortense Spillers, when she observes that during relations under chattel slavery, "whether or not the captive female and/or her sexual oppressor derived 'pleasure' from their seductions and couplings is not a question we can politely ask. Whether or not 'pleasure' is possible at all under conditions that I would aver as non-freedom *for both or either of the parties* has not been settled."[30] Spillers's query loosens the neat connection between the nineteenth-century homosexual and the queer community of the early twenty-first, thereby making their reliance upon pleasure/desire as a defining matrix less edifying, more problematized, and somehow less clearly autonomous as it once seemed.

In this book I intervene at two levels, one academic and one beyond the academy in a historical moment in the United States that wants desperately and unconvincingly to call itself "postracial." On the academic level, I reunite theoretical arguments that, increasingly, have lost touch with one another—as if once upon a time they didn't have a history to share and a future at stake together. As we have seen, these two theoretical stances are critical race theory and queer theory. I am insisting that critical race theory and queer theory must come back together in this moment to resolve key issues and understandings in much the same way that my undergraduate and graduate students insisted that I do in terms of being clear about the connection between the two—a demand that was not always adequately met on my part. When I realized that I had no working roadmap for confluence and/or dissention is the point at which I began the work that became the heart of this project.

While both critical race theory and queer theory have taken a rich and fruitful transnational turn—one that also carries with it a legacy of nonidentitarian, multiple issue layering—in this historical moment, both within academic theory and beyond, I insist that in the erotics of the old black/white binary we understand not only racism but potentially our erotic selves. I am not in any way saying that global understandings don't matter. They do. There are also local, historically situated features of the black/white binary that, in their definitional and oppositional clarity, illuminate our moment and our academic theories in (un)(re)productive ways. This book returns us, ever again, to the black/white binary that many theorists were happy to leave behind. That glee alone should tell us there is unfinished business—but by no means have we forgotten it, solved it, or even, in the end, addressed it. This all-too-brief glimpse takes a look at the structure in which desire and subjugation, belonging and obligation, are linked in theory and practice.

Ultimately, I have not forgotten the details of the scene in that Safeway parking lot, and I never will. In that one hailing denied is embedded an outrageous erotics of racism that in its quotidian expression represents for me an act of profound ontological rupture. A bit of character assassination, for sure, but also an occasion to reflect upon resisting the hailing through its potential for further theorization. What that moment in the parking lot was designed to engender is the spectacular lie of our separation from one another as communities and individuals on this planet. *The Erotic Life of Racism* is an experimental exploration in the denial of that hailing, in the stubborn insistence that we do belong to one another despite our every effort, at home and in the institution, to lose track of, if not forget altogether, such belonging. This book reorders the terrain of critical contact. Because, now as ever, there is no *safe way* but just an ordinary road that we all must travel, I move to the first iteration of the erotic life of racism.

It seems that race, like the presumption of innocence,
the Hippocratic oath, or "till death do us part,"
is too useful a fiction to dispense with.
—Richard Thompson Ford,
"What's Queer about Race?"

"Race" is not what it was.
—Paul Gilroy, *Against Race*

There's No Place like "Beyond"

The rhetorical force of race talk is its ability to invoke that wonderful place called "beyond." If we can divest ourselves of our preoccupation with the past, if we can shed who we are (or have been) to one another, then we can get *beyond* race. Such joyful overcoming is worthy of a civil rights dirge or a Heideggerian tirade on the ends of (human?) history. But as time ticks on, moving *beyond* looks a lot like getting *over*. The particular conundrum here in this desire to move beyond, to get over, race is its reliance upon a future in which we will become, at least discursively, productive. In the wake of Johannes Fabian's classic *Time and the Other: How Anthropology Makes Its Object* (1983), critics such as Lindon Barrett and Michelle Maria Wright have contributed to the further dismantling of the time/space continuum—otherwise known as the West's progress narrative—and the centrality of black bodies to modernity's reimagining of the white self.[1]

As I noted in the introduction, this peculiar overcoming might have its roots in a somewhat pedantic intelligence about the relationship between black and white. It is precisely because the black subject is mired in space and the white subject represents the full expanse of time that the meeting of the two might be thought of as never actually occurring in the same temporal plane; yet the desire to get over such a meeting is immediate and the recovery is often swift. Exactly how does one move *beyond* a nonevent? How can this encounter be so important to us if these two never literally meet? Or to put it another way, maybe my encounter with the woman in the Safeway parking lot attests to the problem of relation—we meet all the time, but like Faulkner's Judith and Henry at Sutpen's Hundred the words we exchange when we happen upon our nonhappening serve as "brief staccato sentences like slaps" that reverberate off the walls, corridors, alleyways, and yes, even parking lots around us.[2] This persistent ordering of such a meeting (one that we usually show up to with script in hand) might lead us to understand the fervent desire to move beyond an encounter that has in fact already occurred in the blood, and yet in time and space remains a nonoccurrence.

The (non)happening, and our critical obsession with its potentiality, marks a strange and schizophrenic approach to the very idea of *relation*. In racist ordering, relation is defined as those who shape time and those who stand outside it, as those who belong to your people, and those who do not. Only grave trespass can produce another order altogether. What makes that parking lot scene so compelling to me is that although my female counterpart certainly wanted to order time for me by manipulating the space I occupied ("move your car please"), she became the one who turned back the clock, thus changing the terms of the relationship. That confrontation illuminates the way in which racist logic ensnares even the racist trying desperately to declare the order of things, verbally or physically. By refusing to move in that Bartleby the Scrivener way—politely, I preferred "not to"—I challenged her to find another way to *move* me. And she did; but not without giving up her own stronghold on time's order of things. To move me she had to situate me in a discourse I would recognize, and in that one moment she looked back past me. Like a rider on a difficult horse, she tried to bring me up under her so that we could move forward—a move that in equestrian parlance equals mastery.[3] In that instance, she touched on the mysterious life force of racist endeavor: in constantly trying to align the world according to a particular ordering, it arrests time rather than attests to its futurity. For her *beyond race* is nothing of the sort—it is just an order of things in which black (radical) yields to white (liberal). Theoretically speaking, *beyond* signals a very dangerous turn for antiracist struggle as it reifies nonrelation while simultaneously *re*inscribing the past (one's history) in a master-slave dialectic. Such is the order of things.

If relation technically happens (two persons, black and white, face to face) but never occurs given the time/space split, then what Eduardo Bonilla-Silva observes holds great purchase on my following review of work in "race" studies. As he notes: "People cannot like or love people they don't see or interact with. This truism has been corroborated by social psychologists, who for years have maintained that friendship and love emerge when people share activities, proximity, familiarity, and status."[4] While reorganizing "status" under capitalism in the United States might be more than a small challenge, it is not difficult to see that proximity and familiarity can create the conditions to overcome racist practice. Or do they? What if proximity and familiarity don't create a level playing field of difference, but instead replicate the terms upon which difference is articulated and therefore maintained? What if our coming together (all the time) is the thing that we continue *not* to see as the lie of nonrelation and difference rolls off our tongues each time we say who we are and where we come from?

In the last two decades of humanities scholarship on race and racism, proponents on either side of an increasingly widening gap have moved through the terrains of racialization as social construction, identity politics, critical race theory, and genetics and genomics in order to understand what constitutes so fraught a belonging.[5] For example, as Antonia Darder and Rodolfo Torres, in their own formulation of racism, announce: "In our analysis 'race,' simply put, is the child of racism."[6] By placing race in pseudo-biological relationship with racism, Darder and Torres metaphorically reify the problem of biological relationship that makes studies of race and racism so difficult to manage. Settling the problem of biological belonging is the psychic life of race, and race work is always already performed by quotidian racism. My project gives depth and shape to the work of racism, arguing first and foremost, as have other Americanists, that racism is not anomalous to quotidian life. The argument here is that racism orders some of the most intimate practices of everyday life, in that racist practice is foundational to making race matter.

Given my earlier preoccupation with (non)relation, I wonder if proximity is the cure for the bad faith of racist practice? In the end, one would wish for more elaboration on Bonilla-Silva's part: What kind of proximity, what level of familiarity? Are we talking "family" here? If one lives and works in a world primarily populated by *phenotypically* white people, proximity slowly morphs into the singularity that is monocular. In this instance whose perspective, whose "see[ing]" will matter most?

Bonilla-Silva's contention about the kind of beneficial work that proximity and familiarity can do is muddied by Jennifer Richeson and J. Nicole Shelton's pioneering work on interracial interaction. Proximity at the level of blood relation does not ensure antiracist practice at all. As Richeson and Shelton find: "Given that interracial contact may be the most promising avenue to prejudice reduction, it is important to examine factors that undermine positive interracial contact experiences, as well as those that facilitate them." In their view, knowing that interracial interactions are cognitively draining is not enough; instead, they suggest "that it is not the goal to control prejudice per se that results in cognitive depletion but, rather, the cognitive processes that individuals employ (i.e., vigilance, suppression, effortful self-presentation) to avoid appearing or behaving in prejudiced ways."[7] This new science about race interaction may be helping us to acknowledge that race may not be on the body, but it certainly is "in" it, as studies such as that of Richeson and Shelton compel us to see certain cognitive machinations as constitutive of the racialized drama we give character to in quotidian life. What *are* we seeing when we see what we see? Are we uploading the same old script and playing our respective parts or are we letting the situation *be*? Are racial encounters the *amor fati* for the twenty-first century?

Where any idea of association—in the bedroom, parking lot, or boardroom—is repudiated, time matters most when the question of descent shackles biology to it. As beings enter into the symbolic and become subjects—the stuff from which personhood is crafted—they enter into a history that literally is not their own; history, in terms of descent, belongs to someone else in the sense that not only is it dependent on those who have come before but also on their place in the racial order—a place that, in turn, defines one's own. Such is the tricky matter of race. As Sonia Sikka, reading Heidegger and his *Volk*, argues: "Descent becomes a determining factor through the way that biology enters 'history'; that is through the inevitable role that it plays in *self*-identification."[8] In the racial order of things, black/white subjects who speak of race connect themselves to the historical in a way that differentiates one history from the other. The purpose here is to maintain the illusion that there is very little shared historico-biological material.

The fact that one has to have a "history" in order to be connected to a people racializes the meaning of "history" and simultaneously locates the idea of being *related* (to someone) to a quotidian progress narrative, one that can be counted by its black and white parts. Here, a rhetoric of "beyond" gives meaning to the meeting of black and white as a nonevent, as the nonevent allows for bloodlines to articulate themselves in a racially ordered fashion. Put more forcefully, Stuart Hall reminds us that "the essentializing moment is weak because it naturalizes and dehistoricizes difference, mistaking what is historical and cultural for what is natural, biological, and genetic. The moment the signifier 'black' is torn from its historical, cultural and political embedding and lodged in a biologically constituted racial category, we valorize, by inversion, the very ground of racism we are trying to deconstruct."[9] Hall's statement demonstrates the problem the historic plays in attempts to both recognize the black body and deploy it as a signifier for something *other than* the biological. He argues for the black body's attachment to the historical, among other categories, by believing that this affiliation is apart from the "biologically constituted." But if to have a history is tied to racial homology, if not feeling, then to think the black body in the historical is to connect it to some trace of its biological force. Such belonging is reiterated in black narratives of community that seem to depend upon the link between bio-logical futurity (generations) as *historical* connection—or in other words the way historical connection is realized is through the biological.

In thinking through this particular beyond—the "reality bites" of critical race studies—it might be fruitful to take some time to consider both where critical energies are focused in the discourse on race and what stories about race *and* racism are consistently rehearsed in that familiar place.

One of my objectives in this chapter is to provide an overview of work in critical race theory that has helped us to arrive at the theoretical crossroads

I have articulated as a meeting between critical race and queer theory. What I outline here is a trajectory for critical race scholarship that has been pivotal in shaping future projects on the nature of race and racism; that contributes in some way to moving my own argument in a particular direction; and that represents some but by no means all of the diversity of work in the field.[10] My hope is that the following redaction will provide an adequate grounding for the intersection I attempt to effect in chapter 3.

Black feminists such as the legal scholar Kimberlé Crenshaw and the political scientist Cathy Cohen draw upon work in gender studies to complicate not only the intersection of conflicting oppressions but also the object of our scholarly inquiry.[11] Crenshaw's "Mapping the Margins: Intersectionality, Identity Politics, and Violence against Women of Color" (1991) is a lengthy exegesis of several cultural, political, and structural narratives in support of her principal claim that critical feminist methodologies about "women" do not apply to the situationality of women of color and black women in particular. Early in her essay, Crenshaw alerts us to the fact that her focus is upon the intersection of gender and race, although, she notes, "class or sexuality are often as critical in shaping the experiences of women of color."[12] While the notion of intersectionality has come under critique as unwieldy and diffuse, and Crenshaw in particular has been criticized for collapsing "black women" into "women of color," the difficulty that the next generation of feminists have with Crenshaw's analysis is not that it attempts to do too much but that it cannot account for sexuality in its framework. Moreover, what intersectionality lacks in Crenshaw's paradigm is a sound methodology to pair with its critique of prevailing assumptions about race and gender.[13] Nevertheless, feminists and critical race scholars have long used her model of the multiple crossings of gender, race, and class, with varying results.[14]

Perhaps the most important contribution to the discourse on race made by Crenshaw's essay is that it was not only a part of early black feminist critiques of poststructuralist thinking, but also that it articulated a way in which social constructionist approaches to theories about race were still useful in scholarly work. As Crenshaw notes: "One rendition of [the] anti-essentialist critique—that feminism essentializes the category of woman— owes a great deal to the postmodernist idea that categories we consider natural or merely representational are actually socially constructed in a linguistic economy of difference. While the descriptive project of post-modernism, of questioning the ways in which meaning is socially con-structed is generally sound, this critique sometimes misreads the meaning of social construction and distorts its political relevance."[15] It is unfortu-nate that Crenshaw's reading here is somewhat tautological—as "meaning" interacts with "social construction" as both origin and byproduct.

Nevertheless, I would like to point out that Crenshaw helps to shape discussions within feminism about the category of woman and essential-ism that reached their peak with the publication of Judith Butler's *Gender Trouble* (1990) thus signaling her engagement with central tenants in femi-nist thought. Crenshaw does follow the arc of black feminist critique—a critique that is thoroughly situated *against* an evacuation of the category of woman for the poststructuralist's linguistic economy of difference. In es-sence, she wants to reserve some room for the *material effects* of social construction. The material effects argument has been very successful in keeping alive the social constructionist position within critical race theory —a position that resists the particular flow of poststructuralism's discur-sivity. For Crenshaw, the social construction of race defines a nuanced politic—one in which ideas about race have material force and therefore phenomenological meaning. In this critical situation we are somewhat betwixt and between: not rid of woman entirely, but not satisfied with her *racial* makeup either.

After Crenshaw's critique of the political saliency of identity, such a position became harder and harder to maintain within queer theorizing, especially as poststructuralism's fragmented body gave way again and again to persistent regulatory regimes so that nothing could be written on or in its changing form. As such, the body's materiality slowly became mere byproduct. What is interesting for my focus in this book is that when the body becomes byproduct—becomes shaped by *discourse*—it moves away from the efforts of critical race scholarship to engage its materiality in a dialectical discourse of "race/racism" and finds itself wholly invested in sexuality. Once Foucault gave the (homosexual) body a history it could reiterate for itself as "the one," not just "a one," the body wrests itself from the same historical trajectory of materiality that life in the Americas de-manded.[16] Gone are the histories of slavery and removal for this frag-mented, discursively besieged body; what is present is the beautiful life awaiting it in the realm of all things queer and possible. Is it at this point that the queer body abandons race?

As if in response to Crenshaw's marginalization of sexuality in the landscape of the intersection, Cathy Cohen's "Punks, Bulldaggers, and Welfare Queens: The Radical Potential of Queer Politics" (1997) attempts to redirect our critical energies in queer studies away from models of respectable objects of inquiry to those who are the most maligned and misunderstood (hence the title). In doing so, she reminds me of the second wave claim that feminism's subject was intended to be the most oppressed woman in society.[17] Cohen's overall strategy is to probe "the disjuncture, evident in queer politics, between an articulated commitment to promoting an understanding of sexuality that rejects the idea of static, monolithic, bounded categories, on the one hand, and political practices structured around binary conceptions of sexuality and power, on the other."[18] Central to Cohen's claim here is a call to reimagine the limits of queer critique—expressed at the boundary between hetero and homo—as an occasion to examine what the formation of a "decentered political identity" might look like.

Inherent in Cohen's interrogation is a demand for queer theory to look to its roots in the social movements of the late 1960s and early 1970s and their discursive rationales for more liberating fodder.[19] In other words, Cohen seems to anticipate the advent of "queer of color critique"—which makes an attempt to ground a queer critical politics in another monolith otherwise known as "women of color feminism," through the figure of the sexual outlaw.[20] Cohen takes seriously Gayle Rubin's claim in "Thinking Sex: Notes for a Radical Theory of the Politics of Sexuality" (1984) that future work in the new sexuality studies would focus upon the most besieged sexual minorities. Both Crenshaw and Cohen represent important shifts for work on race *and* gender, even though many of the critical interventions that followed Crenshaw's article seem to conceive of race as a genderless space, thus skirting the necessity to speak to gender in any comprehensive or meaningful way.[21] Nevertheless, when critics working in critical race theory need to nod toward gendered relations, they find themselves at the doorstep of Crenshaw's work.

Historical materialists such as Robert Miles and Malcolm Brown or social constructionists such as the cultural studies scholar Paul Gilroy would have us understand the importance of race by ridding the critical landscape of this useless fiction. In the case of Miles and Brown, our critical attention is drawn to the invisible and therefore to the mitochondrial war that race, as part of capitalist ideology, wages against oppressed peoples in the name of cultural nationalism.[22] In this instance, a move from the various fictions of race to the work of racism also usually entails the recovery of a class analysis (Miles and Brown) as part of what makes race "work," thus rescuing race from its stranded location on the highway of identity politics. A lack of attention to the importance of a political economy, a class politics in the discourse of race, has driven scholars such as Stuart Hall and Paul Gilroy to challenge those who insist upon the primacy of race in social relations at the expense of "class"—in essence, theirs is a stubborn insistence that economic and political concerns are intertwined.

I group Gilroy with Miles and Brown for two reasons: their roots in British cultural studies and the Centre for Contemporary Cultural Studies, and their importance to one another as interlocutors.[23] Gilroy's most salient contribution to "race" studies can be cited in *Against Race: Imagining Political Culture Beyond the Color Line* (2000). In grappling with identity in particular, he asserts: "Nobody ever speaks of human identity. The concept orients thinking away from any engagement with the basic anti-anthropological sameness that is the premise of this book" (98). By getting away from the particularity of "identity," which harnesses all human action for the benefit of racial and ethnic stereotype and biological difference, Gilroy hopes to arrive at the *human*. Moreover, Gilroy attempts to move us away from our obsession with a "racialized biopolitics" (185), where one's identity is irrevocably attached to the body. While Gilroy's critique has its revolutionary moments, it is still in the social constructionist vein because it posits an afterlife—a beyond—for the body that cannot be sustained by data on race and its material effects. For Gilroy, a "planetary humanism" (17) and "planetary humanity" (356) are absolutely necessary. He urges this move even though "this sharp turn away from African antiquity and toward our planet's future is a difficult and delicate affair, especially if we recognize the possibility that the contested colonial and imperial past has not entirely released its grip upon us" (335). At least in Gilroy's case, we should jettison our reliance upon catastrophic moments of human being for a more apt and futuristic plan; one in which another way of relating would unfold—an anti-anthropological way of being together. Here the beyond and its temporal frame become the nasty buggers that we just cannot escape. After Lucy it looks like African antiquity is indeed our future, not our past.

Gilroy's work is important to my investigation for three reasons: first, he insists upon a "planetary humanism," which echoes a more conservative approach to the discourse on race (the "we are the world" approach); second, he beckons to a "future" that moves against a faction of queer theorizing that holds no brief for the "future"—embodied by the figure of the (racial) child and therefore heteronormative; and third, he depends upon the black/white dichotomy throughout his work to make evidentiary claims about racist practice, a fact that epitomizes the problem that my book seeks to engage.

Gilroy's formula for *beyond* circles back to my earlier contention that it might be time for a reassessment of the survivalist mode for black being—a mode steeped in the often faulty logic of blood, belonging, and family, a trifecta that has not paid off but still has particular resonance within black life and letters. The direction of Gilroy's argument moves against the grain of most critical race work where getting beyond race does not reduce its persistence but only reifies its several fictions (I am thinking here of Derrick Bell's early work in critical race theory). I admit that Gilroy's penultimate remarks are compelling, and I do think that the question remains of how can that movement, that *beyond*, involve a vision of the self that does not include the messy materiality of the body? Or a materiality that mires the body in a location it might not want to occupy?[24] Most importantly, Gilroy seems to be asking whether or not "human" systems along the Western time/space continuum are the only systems that matter. There is a very interesting eco-narrative buried in Gilroy's conclusions, and this is in my view the more profound question that Gilroy poses.

If we want to get beyond the body, why is it that these two bodies (black and white) become the primal scene of racist practice? In other words, while there are a myriad of *racisms* in the world, racist effects are grounded when they become proof of something that whites specifically *do* to blacks. My opening narrative about the incident in the parking lot would seem to solidify this evidentiary paradigm, but I contend that the scene does other work because it is not spectacular but quotidian, and because it speaks to the twisted logic of race that insists that the body's materiality can only be cited in a certain register—that its essence is really only skin deep. My argument moves in the direction of the quotidian because I believe that we have yet to understand just what racist practice is, and focusing on the everyday of the trifecta (blood, belonging, family) mentioned earlier might help to locate a racial politic much closer to home than we have imagined heretofore.

In my mind the parking lot narrative serves to point out the ways in which we are indebted to race's faulty logic—that when we make claims for ourselves and others as racialized beings we invariably put an end to connection and therefore reproduce the very difference that we seek to ameliorate. Gilroy's argument highlights the problematic of "beyond" outlined in this chapter. When we want to think of one race, the human race, then we become insensitive to the very real, very material effects of racist practice; but when we return to that practice, we can only see something produced by the machinations of large systems like the university or the state. We often only have eyes for the spectacularity of racist practice, not its everyday machinations that we in turn have some culpability in. This desire to see ourselves as exempt from racist violence, no matter how small, is part of the same logic that attempts to excise life choices, erotic choices, from these larger systems. What we would have called racism is now "personal choice" or becomes mildly prejudicial. For example, to say that I am not hurting anyone when I say that I prefer to sleep with one racialized being over another, is to tell a different story about the erotic—one where the autonomous becomes clouded by the sticky film of prejudice morphed into quotidian racism. The erotic, therefore, touches upon that aspect of racist practice that cannot be accounted for *as* racist practice but must be understood as something else altogether.

Having jettisoned race as a false category of difference, in their book *Racism* Miles and Brown take a far more practical approach to their articulation of racism by focusing upon the historical emergence of Western nationalisms through capitalism and the importance of racist programs and policies in maintaining the nation-state at the advent of modernity. They eschew "an analysis of racism" in terms of "a phenotypically identifiable victim" and note that "the influence of racism and exclusionary practices is always a component part of a wider structure of multiple disadvantage and exclusion" (17). In particular, they mark the evolution of scholarly work at the Centre for Contemporary Cultural Studies that highlights changes in Britain in the late 1970s and specifically cites a "new racism" emerging from the shift toward a more global, free-market economy and the phenomenon otherwise known through various cultural studies critics, such as Stuart Hall, as "Thatcherism" (61). One could say that the contemporary semantic equivalent for work on "Thatcherism" is the work on neoliberalism by the new American Left, a connection that makes a stronger argument for critical race work in cultural studies as it is broadly defined.[25] No longer tethered by legal restrictions and cultural iconography, racism in the late twentieth century moves to its underground bunker—if it cannot be seen or treated by legal jurisprudence then it simply does not exist. Miles and Brown, moreover, see that focus upon institutionalized racism, specifically in the American context, amounted to the following understanding of the actors in racism's drama: "The dominant and subordinate groups are usually designated by reference to skin colour, as 'whites' and 'blacks' respectively. Consequently, racism is, by definition, effected (intentionally or otherwise) by 'white' people to the disadvantage of 'black' people" (66).

For Miles and Brown this static configuration represents "a significant deflation of the concept of racism" (67).[26] Miles and Brown are important to my project because of the way in which they remind us of the split between American and European conceptualizations of racial formation and its effects.[27] Their explicit contention that racism has been too often considered as something white bodies *do* to black bodies identifies an important break in the transatlantic view of what racism actually is; for Miles and Brown "American" understandings of race rely too often on models of "prejudice" rather than of "power" (70). By casting American understandings of racism as focused on "prejudice" rather than on "power," Miles and Brown are able to interpret the black/white binary as not only situationally archaic but also worthy of our critical contempt. In the wake of arguments like theirs, scholars working at the intersection of queer theory and critical race theory tended to adopt this widely held view—a view that is *constitutive* of the transnational turn in critical discourse. Having thought of all things American as purblind, scholars began to focus on the "larger" picture—a picture in which they themselves play little part. At this stage I want to reiterate that the turn to the transnational as a critical category has been very fruitful to engagements both at "home" and abroad, especially with regard to the extent to which "home" is neither here nor there for many global and migrant populations. What I am pinpointing here is the *psychic life* of that turn and the consequences it has had for studies that focus upon the local rather than the global. Chief among this group would be work in Native studies, which rarely if ever gets taken up by theorists working in the space we now call the "transnational."[28]

By contextualizing the American practice of racism in an archaic view of *racial* history, Miles and Brown inadvertently construct attention to black/white relation as a matter of historical record rather than psychic continuum. Once the black/white dynamic is embedded in a *history*, any appeal to that dynamic creates the condition of backwardness in which negative racialized belonging has been continually mired. In retrospect, Gilroy's call to move "from African antiquity" also produces racist practice as constitutive of a problematic, though noble past. The question here is how to create a new formula for understanding racist practice in a logic in which it exists rather than through a corporeality that we have come to recognize or a history that belongs to it.

Other scholars such as David Theo Goldberg and Philomena Essed join Miles and Brown in challenging scholars in the United States to "face outwards" and move away from a critical race theory mired in "American parochialism."[29] Miles and Brown's critique of the American academy stems largely from a desire to have "a concept of racism that has the ability to grasp and comprehend the diversity of the phenomenon to which it refers" (86). In this appraisal, the black/white binary occludes our vision, preventing us from recognizing that only a few inches away another being is moving down the same stretch.[30]

The charge of "American parochialism" has had a significant impact upon subsequent studies of race and racism in the United States, causing scholars to broaden their inquiries or explain away their inability to do so. It is my contention that this expansion of the discourse to other racisms or other bodies hasn't diminished the need to rethink the black/white binary and its hold upon exemplary epistemologies. This looking "outward," pace Essed and Goldberg, might not be the remedy for our confused racial feeling.

In the final analysis, it is important to note that Miles and Brown are intent upon thinking of racism as *ideology*: "Racism can successfully (although mistakenly) make sense of the world and provide a strategy for political action. It follows that, to the extent that racism is grounded in economic and political relations, strategies for eliminating racism should not concentrate on trying *exclusively* to persuade those who articulate racism that they are 'wrong,' but on changing those particular economic and political relations" (107; emphasis in original). For those scholars who think of racism as ideologically bound, it is necessarily subtended by a set of economic and political relations. While I don't want to refute those claims, I do offer that these sets of relations—economic, political, or otherwise—are attended by a host of perceptions that rupture the binary logic of an ideological paradigm. Quotidian racism in the American tradition might be dependent upon economic and political relations, but it escapes our notice when such relations turn their attention to the procreative possibilities of our erotic lives. In that case, racist action is not only justified but also necessary to prevent slippage into the other—so remarkably *unlike* the self. Racism is phenomenologically bound, but it has exceeded the expectations of the bodies it is attached to; bad faith always cuts in more than one direction when procreative license and practice is at stake. I will think through this constellation of possibilities further in chapter 2.

In contrast to Miles and Brown, the sociologist Eduardo Bonilla-Silva in *Racism without Racists* understands racism as an ideology, but he does not give up on the saliency of the black/white binary, at least in terms of how data are collected. In unpacking the concept of "color-blind racism," Bonilla-Silva focuses upon select data that reveal the justifications by white respondents for discrimination in a post–civil rights era.[31] For Bonilla-Silva, "subscribing to an ideology is like wearing a piece of clothing. When you wear it, you also wear a certain style, a certain fashion, a certain way of presenting yourself to the world."[32] In essence, Bonilla-Silva not only acknowledges that racism, despite our desperate hope, has not disappeared, but that it has a rhetoric, a style through which it survives. In order for this style to be recognized, it has to be reiterated. Moreover, in his review of white attitudes about race and discrimination, he notes that more often than not whites were in the mood to get over the past—and that "past" could usually be represented by the specter of slavery.[33]

One of the primary truths of African Americanist intellectual work is that we are not yet done with slavery—a political stance on the historical that continually thwarts scholarly and well-intentioned efforts to move *beyond* it. Many have mistaken this contention either as evidence of a backward politic—one that specifically runs contrary to an American bootstrap ideology—or as an instance of the primacy of the *black* experience to the exclusion of all others in the historical matrix. This couldn't be further from the truth. I am not proposing here that either of these contentions is unwarranted. Rather, one could only think of "slavery" as specific to the black body if we were to think of it in the narrowest of terms. We are not done with slavery because we have yet to thoroughly investigate its psychic life. This is not to pit the past against the present in a dysfunctional causal relationship (a problematic I pointed out in the introduction to this book). To rethink slavery among us is to take seriously the ways in which its logic of property, belonging, and family reshaped each and every one of those concepts *irrevocably*, as well as the lives of the subjects—black, white, native, Hispanic—who lived within this discursive logic. No one has asked for a return; rather, we have asked for a more thoroughgoing and therefore intellectually challenging way of seeing ourselves—past, present, *and* future.

Despite its progressive agenda, Bonilla-Silva's work still relies on (as almost all qualitative research needs to) the visible divide between black and white to make a point about their (non)relation. How can work that provides an "unrepentant critique" of racism *not* be mired in race as a biological category?[34] After all, how are scholars going to collect the data? We have to start marking categories and making them work for us at the onset, and this process of categorization can be strikingly similar to the work that racism performs for race. *When assessment is on the line, the "races" take their seats at the American feast of difference.*

Perhaps the most important contribution Bonilla-Silva makes is in answer to Michael Omi and Howard Winant's claim in *Racial Formation in the United States* that "blacks can be 'racist' too."[35] Bonilla-Silva posits: "The question needs to be rephrased from 'are blacks as "racist" as whites?' to 'are blacks as "prejudiced" as whites.' I do so because the concept of 'racism' as used by most social scientists and commentators is grounded on methodological individualism (the separation of 'racist' and 'nonracist' individuals) and psychologism (assuming 'racist' individuals are pathological, whereas those who are not 'racist' are normal). In contrast, I have attempted to conceptualize racism as a sociopolitical concept that refers exclusively to racial ideology that glues a particular racial order."[36] At the onset of this paradigmatic shift, Bonilla-Silva returns to the prejudice/power paradigm of Miles and Brown by arguing that racist practice should be reconfigured to "prejudice"—a demotion in every sense of the word. This opts blackness out of racist practice so that the subsequent sentences allude to other bodies. In a sense, in this racial order whites are still racist and blacks simply are prejudiced. Nevertheless, Bonilla-Silva's bold gesture here comes closest to the aims of this project—one that seeks to normalize racism, to move away from "good" or "bad" assessments of its agents (black and white) and toward an understanding of its psychic life and how that life "glues a particular racial order."

The erotic is one particular kind of glue. The attempt here is to cease thinking about that racial order as constitutive of a hierarchy in which whites are on top and blacks are on the bottom—even the more materialist intervention such as Miles and Brown has eschewed such correlation. In chapter 2 I delve into the extent to which one particular set of discussions of the erotic in feminist circles influenced and altered scholarly approaches to the erotic. I am suggesting that a critical reexamination of that process might yield more evidence for *how* racist practice became untethered from the erotic as well as the subsequent critical maneuvers to somehow reattach the thing that was removed from the collective queer body.

What makes race work for us? Why do we need it? In order to push this quotidian exercise toward the work of queer theorizing, I focus on the erotic. The erotic life of racism is the bridge between theories of race and theories of sexuality in all of their diverse complexity. Moreover, by thinking through the erotic—the personal and political dimensions of desire—I differ from Bonilla-Silva in that his reliance upon an ideological ordering for understanding racism still assumes that racism is structured in a particular way. But when in the orbit of racism one cannot help but think about *being* there at all because race talk always wants to be someplace else: beyond black and white ("Can't we all get along?"); beyond the self ("I'm not a racist, but"); beyond the situation ("I wanted to say something, but"). By anchoring the erotic to racist practice, I champion an alternative location for grounding racism—in the quotidian *and* intimate action that brings belonging to one another out into bold relief and perhaps also into question.

I cannot conclude my review of Bonilla-Silva's work without mentioning that for the second edition of *Racism without Racists*, Bonilla-Silva added a penultimate chapter, "*E Pluribus Unum* or the Same Old Perfume in a New Bottle?" to discuss the importance of recent statistics on Latinos being the largest minority group in the country and what significance this might have for our understanding of race and its location in the black/white binary. As he argues:

> The biracial order typical of the United States, which was the exception in the world racial system, is evolving into a complex and loosely organized triracial stratification system similar to that of many Latin American and Caribbean nations. . . . This new order . . . will be apparently more pluralistic and exhibit more racial fluidity than the order it is replacing. However, this new system will serve as a formidable fortress for white supremacy. Its "we are beyond race" lyrics and color blind music will drown the voices of those fighting for racial equality . . . and may even eclipse the space for talking about race altogether. Hence, in this emerging Latin America–like America, racial inequality will remain—and may even increase—yet there will be a restricted space to fight it.[37]

Bonilla-Silva's new conclusions are important to my project because they demonstrate that moving to a multicultural space might not eliminate the problem of race for us all; that "beyond" is a place where achieving a "new order" looks like more of the same. What would moving in the direction of a multicultural space do for our collective understanding of this nation's past? If the conceptualization of the past privileges whiteness as the big-bang theory of the multicultural (that whiteness arrives and therefore makes "races," "difference," etc.) then we are moving toward a "multicultural" society. If that history, however, privileges the presence of diverse Native American cultures in our tale of origin, then the multicultural ground that is our future unmakes a past already seething with multiculturalism's heterogeneity.

The predicament outlined above is precisely why I devote the pages of this book to returning to the binary: just as one would return to a neighborhood that one grew up in because something important happened in that place, and in order to have a "future" one ought to have a fuller and more adequate accounting of the events that took place there. In queer studies the "future" is rendered in the negative because of the championing of queer (male) bodies and their unproductive coupling. The "no future" noted by Lee Edelman that I'd like to posit here fills in the missing piece of this most pervasive form of queer critical engagement—what is that non-productive space looking back upon or forward to? As Edelman offers, "At the heart of my polemical engagement with the cultural text of politics and the politics of cultural texts lies a simple provocation: that *queerness* names the side of those *not* 'fighting for the children,' the side outside the consensus by which all politics confirms the absolute value of reproductive futurism."[38] It is in this unpredictable future that queer meets the race work of *beyond*. If the queer is posited against an agenda of relentless biological warfare then what might beyond, what might the "future," really be gesturing toward? Beyond gets its most trenchant application in Bonilla-Silva's text as the not-so-distant location (the "triracial" event), and its racial diversity prepares us for a further diminishing of the efficacy of scholarly work on race. But shouldn't this happy future provide us with so much more? In my assessment, the purpose of "the future" is to wed us to a particular kind of repetition where the reiteration of past practice enlists both heteronormativity and biological belonging on its side to hide racist endeavor in quotidian practice. The racial event embedded in the process of biology's search for a future entails some critique of the networks of racial belonging and power that subtend such avid seeking.

I want to return to the system of white supremacy that Bonilla-Silva implicitly engages and that critical race work seeks to understand. Bonilla-Silva thinks of white supremacy as "racialized social systems" that "became global and affected all societies where Europeans extended their reach" and therefore takes for granted its acknowledged presence among us.[39] There is great debate in historiography (Barbara Fields, in particular) as to when Euro-supremacy became "white" supremacy. I can think of no better articulation of the presence of "white supremacy" among us than Charles Mills's analysis of the "social contract." Mills begins *The Racial Contract* with the following startling observation:

White supremacy is the unnamed political system that has made the modern world what it is today. You will not find this term in introductory, or even advanced, texts in political theory. A standard under-graduate philosophy course will start off with Plato and Aristotle, perhaps say something about Augustine, Aquinas, and Machiavelli, move on to Hobbes, Locke, Mill and Marx, and then wind up with Rawls and Nozick. It will introduce you to notions of aristrocracy, democracy, absolutism, liberalism, representative government, social-ism, welfare capitalism, and libertarianism. But though it covers more than two thousand years of Western political thought and runs the ostensible gamut of political systems, there will be no mention of the basic *political system* that has shaped the world for the past several hundred years. And this omission is not accidental.[40]

In this dramatic opening, Mills reminds me of my own experience in a standard introductory philosophy and literature course at Princeton University and takes me to the unanswered questions seeking refuge in words like "genius" and "merit" and "great books." Why do some of the most influential works of Western thought say so little about white power as a political system? In thinking of white supremacy as "based on a 'contract' between whites, a Racial Contract," Mills remakes the social contract de-vised by Hobbes, Locke, Rousseau, and Kant.[41] A critique of Mills's posi-tion here could rest on a reliance upon happenstance (Europeans hap-pened to be white and, ergo, white supremacy) as biological imperative. This kind of thinking leads us to believe that if only "we" were in power then things would be different, even though "history" tells another story (I am thinking here of Cherokee slavery or the Israeli occupation of Pal-estine, for example). What if human overcoming were simply a way to ignore questions of systemic planetary abuse, for example? (a question that lurks in Gilroy's earlier remarks).

The larger question here is beyond the scope of this study, but I do think that Mills's conceptualization is both eye opening and beautifully disas-trous, because at the end of the day the racialized aspect of "white" su-premacy uncovers something more pernicious in its wake: namely, the extent to which acts of quotidian differentiation can normalize racist en-deavor.[42] The question here is not who is doing it, or how, but rather why racial differentiation is necessary at all and when it is, what system (already in place) might it be participating in?

By identifying white supremacy as a political system, Mills calls our attention to the kinds of detrimental *civilizing* effects that pollute notions of political and cultural terms such as "manifest destiny" or the "New World." In addition, Mills makes a different historical genealogy matter— one that Foucault, for all of his attention to biopower, to turning the human into a regulated and regulatory entity, seems to neatly omit; one that is instrumental to the production of narratives of citizenship, belonging, and that twenty-first-century truism called "nation building." Nevertheless, what is useful in Mills's assessment of white supremacy is his emphasis on *epistemological* force, as it has a way of "prescribing norms for cognition to which its signatories must adhere."[43] This is where Mills's findings pair well with those of Richeson and Shelton—where modes of cognition produce a certain kind of race work, albeit often unseen.

Mills's other important contribution to the discourse about (white) racism is his insistence upon the centrality of race to Western ideals and its importance in a nascent dialectic. Mills seems to move against the grain of discourse on race by observing that race rather than a developmental outcome of Western expansion is "in no way an 'afterthought,' [or] a 'deviation'" from those ideals but rather constitutive of them.[44]

Historians and political theorists seem to have reached some consensus about the Enlightenment's take on race; a consensus that involves seeing the Enlightenment's increasing focus on race as a growing out of more religious or national concerns. In sum, critics often prefer a gradualist approach to understandings of the Enlightenment, and they claim that race develops as a distinct category and becomes a biopolitic when the social sciences emerge as disciplines and succeed in cementing "the body as the locus of identity and difference."[45] Mills's difference from prevailing understandings of the Enlightenment project is expressed methodologically: his view on race and the racism it engenders is steeped in analytical rather than continental philosophy.[46]

Nevertheless, one important example of this gradualist approach to Enlightenment race theory is outlined in Thomas Gossett's early work on race: "The importance of Negro slavery in generating race theories in this country can hardly be overestimated, but it must be remembered that there was a minimum of theory at the time the institution was established. The theory of any political or social institution is likely to develop only when it comes under attack, and the time for opposition to slavery was still far in the future."[47] While Gossett's oppositional paradigm might not be the best trigger for antiracist action, the feminist theorist Robyn Wiegman offers one articulation of the encumbered landscape of racial formation.[48] In her analysis of the role of new technologies such as camera obscura in the making of what would come to constitute the visual or *knowledge* about the visual, she provides some cautionary remarks: "We would be wrong to assume that the motivating force of natural history was to establish scientific proof for white supremacy in a theory of multiple creations."[49] Wiegman's emphasis on the classification and therefore differentiation of bodies is mirrored in Mills's later assessment of the Racial Contract as something that "makes the white body the somatic norm."[50] In essence, Mills's quest is to get at the *materiality* of moral reason, while Wiegman's point is to think through how that materiality produces and subtends knowledge about a subject or, for that matter, a field of inquiry. In returning to the "how" of interaction, and perhaps moving away from the analytical to the phenomenological, Mills asserts that "*on matters related to race, the Racial Contract prescribes for its signatories an inverted epistemology, an epistemology of ignorance, a particular pattern of localized and global cognitive dysfunctions (which are psychologically and socially functional), producing the ironic outcome that whites will in general be unable to understand the world they themselves have made.*"[51] Mills's insistence upon the (benign) social contract as in fact a racial contract also does other work here—it transforms the singularity of rationality at the center of the Western episteme, and as a consequence redefines racism as a very rational act.[52] Racist action *makes* the system of racial differentiation work. What is useful to my project is that Mills's work allows for racist action to come into the quotidian—a move that puts his work solidly within critical race theory's critical trajectory.

As if to prove my claims that talk of race is always already laced with a strange temporality, neither here nor there but always with us, Wiegman offers the following: "If rethinking the historical contours of Western racial discourse matters as a political project, it is not as a manifestation of an other truth that has previously been denied, but as a vehicle for shifting the frame of reference in such a way that the present can emerge as somehow less familiar, less natural in its categories, its political delineations, and its epistemological foundations."[53] Where the present can be rearticulated for what it is, and where what it is—its cognitive life—can be rendered like fat through its epistemological foundations, then this might be the place where Wiegman and Mills meet.[54]

As a feminist scholar Wiegman's goal is to see how such supremacy works in concert with racist and sexist practice. As she writes: "The productive function of the discourse of sexual difference as an increasingly deployed mechanism of racial signification and control attaches in ways to black male bodies that are crucial to a feminist politics of antiracist struggle—to a feminist politics that is not simply invested in bringing back the black woman into critical view, but which traces the historical and theoretical contexts that shape her absence and that speak more broadly to the intertwining relationship between patriarchy and white supremacy."[55] Wiegman's attention to gender (a category that lacks illumination in Mills's text)[56] in the complex matrix of race/sex/sexuality/class has important implications for this project, as my goal here is to return to that nexus that critics acknowledge profoundly shapes postmodern understandings of who we are and how we interact, yet a nexus they profoundly misread or undertheorize. Like Wiegman, the chapters that follow in this book ultimately focus upon how we have lost the black (lesbian) body. In my focus here, however, I do not argue that this erasure is produced by patriarchy and white supremacy. Instead, I understand this disappearance as also necessary to a certain mode of queer theorizing that cannot account for itself without that body's erasure—even in its precise moment of absolutely recognizing and inscribing it.

This review of critical race theory would not be complete without a nod to the work by practitioners of postpositive realism. Satya Mohanty, Paula Moya, and Michael Hames-García, among others, articulate their project as an attempt to engage the fault lines of postmodernism's critique of constructivism by offering a critical alternative wherein we can see the inherent value in experience while simultaneously retaining objectivity, and rejecting, in the words of Mohanty, "as overly abstract and limiting this conception of objectivity as presupposition-free knowledge." By "understand[ing] multiculturalism as a theory of social justice" and defining multiculturalism "as a form of epistemic cooperation across cultures," Mohanty and his critical allies move the discussion about race away from the zero sum game of "us vs. them" and toward a *grounding* in identity that cannot be easily assailed from the vantage point of a colorblind neoliberalism.[57] The epistemic significance of identity and the importance of multiculturalism to the postpositivist realist project are more thoroughly outlined in Moya's *Learning from Experience*.[58] Mohanty lodges his critique in the same political theory as Mills, but their faith in its applicability and even universality differs greatly. While I am not convinced by postpositivist realist claims about *multicultural* possibility, that project has usefulness for this study because of its emphasis upon emotion. In paraphrasing the work of the philosopher Naomi Scheman, Mohanty surmises that "our emotions provide evidence of the extent to which even our deepest personal experiences are socially constructed, mediated by visions and values that are 'political' in nature, that refer outward to the world beyond the individual."[59] Mohanty gestures toward the very same province of emotion—let's call this "racial feeling"—that I seek to unpack in this book. This shift toward "emotion" has critical manifestations in work on "public feelings," bodily affect, and performance, and it is my hope that what I touch upon here will add to that conversation but in an unfamiliar register. It is to this psychic life of emotion—volatile and pleasurable—that I now turn.

DESIRE

or "A Bit of the Other"

Kwame Anthony Appiah tells us, "In our private lives, we are morally free to have aesthetic preferences between people, but once our treatment of people raises moral issues, we may not make arbitrary distinctions."[1] Writing in another time, Emmanuel Levinas asks, "Is the Desire for the Other (*Autrui*) an appetite or a generosity?"[2] These two quotes exist in relationship to one another, as Appiah's excuse for the ego's embarrassing commitments are relegated to "aesthetic preference" and Levinas's equivocation between appetite and generosity speaks to the means rather than the ends of such commitments. At issue here is whether or not aesthetic preference *ever* passes as proper moral practice.[3] Since Appiah's words are grounded in his study of "racisms" and Levinas's are not, it would seem a bit of a stretch to hold them in conversation with one another. But the words "appetite" and "generosity" are compelling here, and their use for a discourse about racism and its erotic life could be quite generative. In reading the words "appetite" and "generosity" together, one could surmise that what we need to do is turn an appetite—an "aesthetic preference"—into an antiracist stance; a "generosity" that has great potential. Let us suppose that where the error occurs for Appiah is when our motivational energy turns what is aesthetic differentiation into a moral absolute. But what if such a beginning is always already flawed? What if that little thing called individual preference is the sounding moment for racist desire? How can one unmake the (queer) autonomy of desire—the thing that is shaped, like many other emotions, and circumscribed by the racist culture that we live in?[4] How can one disarticulate a personal preference from a racist attitude? When does a simple preference become an absolute?[5] Appiah's formulation harbors a contradiction, since what was once "aesthetic preference" *becomes* an "arbitrary distinction" only when treatment of people raises moral issues. A personal preference can become morally reprehensible when the private becomes public. This split between private and public, personal and political, has been soundly critiqued by feminist scholars and queer scholars, notably by Michael Warner in his searing examination of America's obsession with sex, shame, and censure in *The Trouble with Normal: Sex, Politics and the Ethics of Queer Life* (1999). In essence, distinctions are okay so long as they remain in the realm of the personal (not always political perhaps), but when members of the group become cognizant of their precarious desires, there is a moral imperative to bring them in line with accepted standards of behavior.

My premise here is that we have uncoupled our desire from quotidian racist practice for far too long. What follows in the next section is an examination of that uncoupling and how it might have been wrought over time and space. Much of the conversation about "the erotic" has taken place under the auspices of sexuality studies. I now turn to that discourse to map some of its key players since Gayle Rubin's groundbreaking essay "Thinking Sex: Notes for a Radical Theory of the Politics of Sexuality" (1984)—an essay that helped to "birth" at least two genealogies of queer studies work: one trajectory organized by Halperin, Warner, Bersani, and Edelman, and the other organized by Butler, Sedgwick, Halberstam, and Halley. I note these players on the field because the majority of the writers in queer studies feel the need to address or cite the contributions of these queer studies scholars in some form or other. The gendered divide is alarming here as work in one order of queer studies sees the body as consistently under attack by both regulatory regimes and the symbolic order, while the other mode of queer address focuses on persistently calling into question the body's situationality.

In speaking about the racist prohibition embedded in the binary between black and white, Marlon Ross observes that "the black-white polarity enables Americans to continue to deny the polymorphous course of all human desire. Giving Americans a screen for projecting fear, this polarity prevents them from dealing directly with the unclassifiable, uncolored course of desire itself."[6] For Ross, racist prohibition prevents "human desire" from working its steady magic. Like Gilroy, Ross imagines the realm of (queer) desire as an "uncolored course," enlisting the category of the human to provoke us into seeing how unencumbered desire should and could be. I am very much in support of this claim; however, what I propose to unveil is how desire became so autonomous in queer theory and why claims to some universal humanity, though laudable, do not quite capture the kind of complex and often pernicious work that a "black-white polarity" does for us both critically and in everyday practice.

It is my contention here that racist practice *does* limit human desire by attempting to circumscribe its possible attachments—a point I argued in the introduction to this book. Here I pose that there is no "raceless" course of desire, and I do so to ascertain the practiced nature of quotidian racism and how those practices shape what we know of as "desire." In other words, this work might attempt to answer the question posed by Michael Hames-García in "Can Queer Theory Be Critical Theory?": "To what extent can the privileging of desire as a realm of freedom and/or transgression [within queer studies] occlude the collusion of desire with domination and oppression?"[7]

While queer materialist scholars have examined desire's "collusion" with domination and oppression, there has been little work on how the psychic life of racism might have its erotic, desiring components. Elizabeth Freeman comes close to my observations here in her creation of the term "erotohistoriography," which she claims is "a politics of unpredictable, deeply embodied pleasures that counters the logic of development" and "indexes how queer relations complexly exceed the present."[8] Freeman's presentation of desire is so *capable* that it can even remaster "the logic of development," as it is articulated through a paradigm of past/present/future. Unlike its erotic counterpart—cast as exceeding the boundaries of duration—racism consistently embeds us in a "past" that we would rather not remember, where time stretches *back* toward the future, curtailing the revolutionary possibilities of queer transgression. Freeman's configuration moves us away from Edelman's celebration of queer futurity's lack and centers the critique upon a capricious nonlinearity—or to be more precise, an exacting and disabling recursivity that appears like a scene from *Waiting for Godot*.[9]

It is my pledge in this book to find the admittedly tenuous although nonetheless compelling connection between the erotic and racism. My work on the erotic moves the boundary of the understanding of desire by queer studies from the province of an abstract and autonomous desire toward the materiality of the everyday, while simultaneously maintaining attention to queer studies' inheritance from feminist inquiry.[10] While I do not promise an explicit critique of *capital*, I am indebted to scholars such as Rosemary Hennessy who have taken it upon themselves to think through the relationship between capitalism and sexuality. In one of the most salient critiques of Rubin's groundbreaking "Thinking Sex," Hennessy offers the following view: "When desire is understood as lust, where lust is equated with a basic human drive, its historical production becomes invisible. More to the point of my argument, invocations of lust as a natural experience to which women have a right can limit our thinking about human agency, including sexual agency, to individual terms and so forestall the possibility of linking this aspect of human life and agency to a more collective endeavor. Desire remains abstracted and reified, and so we are also not enabled to see that this particular form of desire is not even available to all women."[11]

Like Michael Hames-García, Hennessy cautions us to rethink the radicalism in which queer desire is so awash. While her alignment of desire with "lust" might seem almost prudish, the materialist feminist vocabulary that Hennessy utilizes necessitates viewing desire as historically produced. For the most part, queer theory's sense of historically produced desire gets its most salient critique in Halperin's essay "Is There a History of Sexuality?" By thinking through erotic connections between peoples in classical Athens as manifestations of power through various forms of state *citizenship*, Halperin is able to question our preconceived notion of what a history of sexuality might look like. Therefore, Hennessy's insistence that desire is historically produced has special salience *both* inside of the Marxist lexicon from which she draws and for my earlier contention that history matters, but its organization and alignment of bodies within its discursive boundaries can detract from fuller explications of how bodies actually work, move, and interact. My claims about history here and elsewhere have their precursor in Linda Hart's work on lesbian s/m. Focusing her critique on Linda Wayne's observations about the display of symbols "particularly fascist imagery" representing historical atrocities, Hart observes: "While I myself, like many other pro-s/m lesbians, found it extremely difficult to accept the wearing of such symbols, Wayne is, I think, right to point out that to view them as static representations, iconographically and inextricably linked to acts that they once signified, contributes to their power to represent these acts as if they are *outside history*. That is not to say that what they have represented is not historical, but it does seem to suggest that this history has obtained a certain static, immutable quality, a timelessness."[12] As I argue in this book, representations of the historical have gotten in the way of our ability to see black/white relation in anything but static terms.

Having a right to our queer desires is a fundamental tenet of queer theorizing, and Hennessy problematizes this theoretical arrangement—an arrangement that, as we shall see here and in the next chapter, has its black and white parts. By abstracting desire, notes Hennessy, queer theory detaches it from lived experience—especially the lived experience of women. Unlike Butler, Rubin, and others Hennessy does find space to address "women," and so her project holds a brief for feminist critique by not foreclosing as theoretically bankrupt our ability to speak to the condition of women as a category. Moreover, Hennessy's valuation of "desire" attaches it to "a more collective endeavor"—an endeavor I see as holding out the possibility for racism's rhetorical return to the landscape of the erotic. Again, we are called to remember the public and private, personal and political, and this collective quickly becomes politicized and oddly black and white the more that critiques of queer theory's center abound.

In addition, it is important to note that in this project I am very aware of how the erotic is tied to notions of blackness, and race *as* blackness.

Blackness, at least as it is understood in visual culture, not only produces "erotic value" for whiteness,[13] but it holds the very impossibility of its own pleasure through becoming the sexualized surrogate of another. In a sense, *blackness can never possess its own erotic life*. Scholars on "blackness" such as Hortense Spillers and Saidiya Hartman have contributed to the Fanonian concept of blackness as the thingness of the thing by arguing for a more absolute abjection under slavery and colonization—an abjection that places the black body in peril and, for Hartman at least, even in the midst of somewhat quotidian scenes of pleasure.[14] My explorations at the boundary between black and white attempt to unmake this foregone conclusion. While queer studies might believe that desire always produces or makes "difference," even violently so (I'm thinking of Bersani reading Lacan here), the shape and texture of that "difference" is usually defined within the limits of queer theory's appropriate object—sexuality. To reiterate: in thinking through the erotic my project is guided by work in queer theory but not grounded in its usual set of critical investments. Ultimately I attempt something rather inappropriate, if not uncomfortable; namely, I suggest that we can't have our erotic life—a desiring life—without involving ourselves in the messy terrain of racist practice. To think through this connection—how we uncoupled racism and the erotic and how we rearticulate the connection—I now move back in time to our thorny feminist inheritance.

QUEER PHENOMENON

In the last decade or so feminist critics and philosophers have been resurrecting and reinterpreting Simone de Beauvoir's existentialism—notably her intellectual departure from Sartre and contribution to his work; the faulty translation by H. M. Parshley of her seminal work *The Second Sex*; and her various influences across the disciplines.[15] The chief component of Beauvoir's oeuvre is an acceptance of the erotic as a philosophical category —an allowance that stems from her work with phenomenological concerns. Her claims culminate in *The Second Sex*, which among other things establishes a feminist ethic of the erotic. The kind of meaning that Beauvoir alludes to in the erotics of all psychic relationships is very similar to Audre Lorde's later conceptualization of the term. In speaking of the erotic, Beauvoir advances the following observations: "The erotic experience is one that most poignantly reveals to human beings their ambiguous condition; they experience it as flesh and as spirit, as the other and as the subject." She continues as follows: "There is in eroticism a revolt of the instant against time, of the individual against the universal: to try to channel and exploit it risks killing it, because live spontaneity cannot be disposed of like inert matter; nor can it be compelled in the way a freedom can be."[16] What Beauvoir finds in the erotic is rooted in the revolutionary potential for a certain autonomy. This revolutionary potential is constitutive of an *autonomy* that tends to drive much of early queer studies work— the erotic is risky for the whole because it focuses exclusively on the *individual* by breaking an individual off from the regulatory structures that make community, place, and home while simultaneously casting the queer subject over and against such normative spaces.[17] For Beauvoir, the erotic is a good thing because it quite simply allows women in particular to possess their own sexuality. If the erotic cannot be "compelled in the way a freedom can be," then it rests in a plane apart from other and perhaps more pernicious desires. But what if our erotic selves have been compelled not just by state intervention but also by such terms as "community," "home," and "race"?[18]

The erotic thus recalls the impossibility of community with *an*other, mocking our ability to connect, and also highlights the reciprocal nature of subjectivity, or what it means to be a subject—as subjectivity is constituted not so much from a belief in the self and one's own actions but in the understanding of another with whom we have connection (hell *is* the other, after all). The life of the erotic is cradled in the definition of what it means to be human in the first place, and in the second ordering of the erotic through eroticism it contextualizes for Beauvoir the pleasure and danger of *women's sexuality*, specifically.[19] As if to capitalize on the fruitfulness of this philosophical predicament while still holding out hope for Beauvoir's brief for the *female* subject, Lorde remarks that "the erotic is a resource within each of us that lies in a deeply female and spiritual plane . . . firmly rooted in the power of our unexpressed or unrecognized feeling."[20] The capacity of this "feeling" and our need to pay attention to it could easily be recognized in the spate of theoretical discourse on "public feelings" and "affect"—discourses that implicitly align themselves with early feminist musings about the unexpressed or the unrecognized.

Lorde's work on the erotic in "Uses of the Erotic: The Erotic as Power" was delivered twenty-six years (1978) and published over thirty years (1984) after Beauvoir's *The Second Sex* was first published in 1952. It expresses a commitment not only to the erotic but also to a *gendered* erotic; one harnessed by and for women: "The principal horror of any system which defines the good in terms of profit rather than in terms of human need, or which defines human need to the exclusion of the psychic and emotional components of that need—the principal horror of such a system is that it robs our work of its erotic value, its erotic power and life appeal . . . reduc[ing] work to a travesty of necessities, a duty by which we earn bread or oblivion for ourselves and those we love."[21] Both Beauvoir and Lorde indicate an investment in the erotic for its potential to undermine pre-existing notions of the self (woman's self) and society. This conceptual-ization of the erotic is constitutive of phenomenological work from Hus-serl to Sartre, Merleau-Ponty to Levinas, and although a rich appraisal of this trajectory would be fascinating, it would take us beyond the specific purpose of this book. From the dialectical to the transcendental to being itself, the remnants of phenomenology's claim upon the queer studies project can be seen everywhere—as sexuality can potentially mark the signal event that moves the old Cartesian contest between self/society into the intimate space of the bedroom, thereby pulling us into the contest of self/other/self at play and calling for a rearticulation of our relations, public and private.[22]

In this regard, phenomenology's stake in the personal *and* the political finds its most comfortable adaptation in the work of queer studies, an adaptation that fuels claims against the apparent myopia of queer studies— a myopia that queer of color critique and to some extent black queer studies attempt to redress. Sara Ahmed's *Queer Phenomenology* is an adept reimagining of phenomenology's utility for a queer studies project on the body in time and space. In it she notes, through a reading of Fanon, that phenomenology tends to orient itself on the surface of things. She sees Fanon as a counter to the depthlessness of phenomenological claims: "Fanon asks us to think of the 'historic-racial' scheme . . . the racial and historical dimensions are beneath the surface of the body described by phenomenology which becomes, by virtue of its own orientation, a way of thinking the body that has surface appeal" (110). While I am respectful of this almost postpositivist attempt to make race matter—to have those so-cial relations that express racial feeling matter to the surface schema that is phenomenology's contribution to the table of ideas about perception and consciousness—I am not wholly convinced that the inside/outside or surface/depth paradigms serve us well here.

One other contribution to the discussion of surface is Jay Prosser's meticulous assessment of that very surface and its absenting of the trans-sexual body. In arguing very persuasively that "just below the surface" of the foundational texts in sexuality studies is the transgendered body, Pros-ser critiques *trans* as the ultimate metaphor for queer's postmodern fluid-ity and performative movement. For Prosser, queer theory is so indebted to the surface model of subjectivity—discourse on the body but not *in* it—that the materiality posed by the *transsexual* body cannot and ought not to be read as part of the same matrix.[23] All of this talk of *racial* and *trans* being beneath the surface points toward an embeddedness in the flesh with which my project is uncomfortable.

Materiality is a beautiful thing, but when it is marked by the historical in such a way that one has to provide a certain (and often delimiting) narra-tive to legitimize and make legible the body's presence (think of the scene in the Safeway parking lot that opens this book) then we run the risk of treating history as essence rather than as one narrative among many. Pros-ser does, however, attempt to correct this problem of the historical by creating an alternative archive, thus utilizing transsexual narratives as fod-der for understanding the body's materiality. His study is important to my project because its investment in the flesh doesn't always rely upon the historical dimensions of materiality to write the human being for us. But the material effects of erotic investments are not always so tangible as racist effects seem to be, or are they?

I return briefly to one moment in Ahmed's text that dovetails with the penultimate analysis in this chapter as I seek to unpack as well as compli-cate the codependent relationship between racist practice and desire. In defining the directional motivations of colonialism, Ahmed offers the fol-lowing reformulation: "The 'direction' of the social wish is for access, and this 'direction' also makes others accessible . . . It is not that nations have simply directed their wishes and longings toward the Orient but rather that the nation 'coheres' an effect of the repetition of this direction. . . . Such repetition is not innocent but strategic: the direction of such wishes and longings makes others available as resources to be used, as the materials out of which collectives might 'write' themselves into existence."[24] The fine line between source and *re*source is not necessarily the political power of a state apparatus, but rather the trained disciplinary matter of an intellectual inquiry. In critical practice we have seen time and again how "women of color" or "race" are reiterated as strategic categories of difference; their deployment speaks volumes about the resourcefulness of discursive endeavors.

For Ahmed, bodies are a centrifugal force—they "tend toward" as much as they pull others in. Clearly the focus upon desire—the erotic of Lorde and Beauvoir to some extent—is important in the process of orientation under colonialism, as desire (longing) marks the place of colonial *access*, thus turning the desired one into a kind of melancholic digestif. You can attempt to incorporate *it* all you want to, but the thing you want will remain forever elusive, so you must try to capture it in other ways—fixing it through law (the condition of the child shall follow the condition of the mother in the United States context) and custom (the overall perception that the idea of a "neighborhood" reflects cultural ebb and flow rather than racist practice). The spatiality of affective relations outlined by Ahmed changes both the direction and the definition of desire itself. Here, the erotic is less like autonomous life and more connected to a matrix of desiring relations that tend to make it difficult to mark where racist (here, colonial) practice begins and where our good desire ends.[25] *Is the desire for another an appetite or a generosity?* Whether appetite or generosity, *desire* in queer theory in the twenty-first century holds no brief for "women" and the host of materialist concerns that come with her writ large.

Beauvoir's and Lorde's work on the erotic is punctuated by what feminists have come to think of as essentialist claims about the "nature" of the feminine and female experience, although the new renaissance in Beauvoir studies has tried to provide a more nuanced understanding of her contributions to feminist inquiry by interrogating the charge of essentialism against her. In any event, Lorde and Beauvoir want to claim for "women" a particularized purchase upon their experience. In recent years, it has become almost impossible to speak for or about women within emerging feminist/queer theorizing because of the call to a *subjectless* feminism—

first put forth by Butler in *Gender Trouble*, rearticulated in her essay in *differences* "Against Proper Objects" (1994), and cited across a spectrum of critical texts.[26] Sonia Kruks's review essay of Beauvoir criticism notes that Sara Heinämaa's investigation of Beauvoir's work sees value in her focus on the *lived experience* of women—a focus that is not the same thing as essentializing them. Moreover, it is clear in Heinämaa's reevaluation of Beauvoir's place within phenomenology that the purpose of her study is to break us of the habit of seeing Beauvoir in Sartre's shadow. To this end, Heinämaa's work is a major reconsideration of Beauvoir's oeuvre. More to the point, she demonstrates the extent to which Butler's early work on feminist philosophy was engaged in a concerted dismantling of Beauvoir's essentialist existentialism.

For example, one can see evidence of the feminist debate over Beauvoir's legacy in the text and footnotes of *Gender Trouble*. In one instance Butler remarks, "Note the extent to which phenomenological theories such as Sartre's, Merleau-Ponty's, and Beauvoir's tend to use the term *embodiment*. Drawn as it is from theological contexts, the term tends to figure 'the' body as a mode of incarnation and, hence, to preserve the external and dualistic relationship between a signifying immateriality and the materiality of the body itself."[27] As with much of philosophical writing, we are directed in both Butler and Heinämaa to a fundamental misreading of the philosophical texts at issue so that in the end it is hard to say which reading might be exact(ing) enough to merit our collective attention. My own reading of Heinämaa's work sees that again and again in Beauvoir and in critical evaluations of her work, race is set apart from sexed embodiment since— for Kruks as well—all societies do not necessarily make racial distinctions. But this works only if we know to what "race" or the "racial" actually refer. In reading this reassessment of Beauvoir I am reminded of how the racialized subject is lost in the play of desire, flesh, consciousness, and transformation—how the body *appears* to another and how it is *historicized* makes it legible (to critics) and therefore determines its relationship to the philosophical question at hand.[28] Philosophy can only see black/white subjectivity in a historical interface where blackness is denied access to a white social contract or where whiteness determines the limit of the law. Have we really begun to see (black) white subjects as racialized beings within a framework that doesn't lose them to a white supremacy that looks more and more like something out of the blinding whiteness that concludes Shelley's *Frankenstein*?

BLACK BODIES, BLACK FEMINISMS

If race is a mark on the body that is nonnegotiable—under the skin and on the surface—then what do we do with *it*? In essence, how can philosophy account for the lived experience of a body it has, in the words of Heinämaa, "failed to think and imagine," or a body it has failed to think or imagine in any but static ways?[29] How can you make appear the thing that is necessary to *disappear* in order for the work of philosophical inquiry to commence? Each of these questions points to the way in which the body is imagined as the grounding figure for the creative origins of philosophical thought. For the most part, whenever neoliberal thought wants to think about the body of color, this figure is deployed through a historical matrix that mires the racially embodied in one particular historical dynamic. The dialectic produced from this dynamic imposes transcendent being for the one and historical meaning for the other. This conundrum is very similar to the one that Mills poses in *The Racial Contract*—how can philosophical inquiry account for the invisible (to itself) system of white supremacy? By thinking through our erotic commitments, we might come to think differently about the historical—we might find a grounding for racist practice that acknowledges both systemic practices *and* quotidian effects that far exceed our patterned understanding of how history has happened to us.

Ironically, Simone de Beauvoir might be one of the few philosophers to pay some attention to New World slavery in her accounting of women's oppression, although that attention is made through a problematic analogy. As Margaret Simons argues in *Beauvoir and "The Second Sex*," Beauvoir understands that "the master and slave, engaged in human activities, are, in Beauvoir's view, essentially similar and yet radically dissimilar to woman, who is confined to a lower, animal-like life" (25). The problem here is really with the category of the human rather than that of the slave, as Simons continues: "A major problem with this comparison between slavery and women's oppression lies in Beauvoir's characterization of slavery. In the American slavery experience, which Beauvoir refers to extensively, justifications for slavery relied upon racist ideology espousing the animal-like character of the slaves. Instead of being seen as essentially similar to their masters, slaves were perceived as radically dissimilar. Slaves were thus confined to the category of the 'Other' in racist ideology, as women were in sexist ideology" (26). This is a common opposition, and one that was much critiqued by feminist scholars in the 1980s and even into the 1990s.[30] But I do not believe that we have left behind this useful formulation, as reconstituting the black/white binary as woman of color versus queer theory (at least in queer of color critique), does nothing to loosen the ties that bind blackness to a particular historical accounting. This kind of theorizing draws and quarters black.female.queer in an unrelenting logic of forgetting and displacement that is still being played out in contemporary theorizing. I shall engage this body of thought in the next chapter.

A few pages later in her book, Simons reviews feminist criticism from the 1970s and notes that "one is struck by the relative lack of attention given to racism and the oppression of minority women" (28). Racism is something done to "minority women" rather than a practice affecting all "women" in the larger culture. Unfortunately, Simons relies upon the same representational dichotomy that has dogged mainstream feminism and sparked the publication of *All the Women Are White, All the Men Are Black, But Some of Us Are Brave*—a critique of the "proper object" of critical (feminist) inquiry that emerged long before Butler's queries in *Gender Trouble*. To narrow this problem somewhat, I ask how do we get past (get over?) the exasperating static situation of the (black) female body? History includes the doers and the done to, so that seeking refuge in historical situationality doesn't do much to remind us that something called "black feminism" is always already at the table of feminist ideas.

In Lorde's "Uses of the Erotic"—the most thoroughgoing (black) feminist engagement with the erotic—she proposes that we siphon off our erotic self from its opposite, the pornographic. As she writes: "The erotic has often been misnamed by men and used against women. It has been made into the confused, the trivial, the psychotic, the plasticized sensation. For this reason, we have often turned away from the exploration and consideration of the erotic as a source of power and information, confusing it with its opposite, the pornographic. But pornography is a direct denial of the power of the erotic, for it represents the suppression of true feeling. Pornography emphasizes sensation without feeling" (54). This is one of the most important feminist statements in the latter part of the twentieth century.[31] In my view, it places the most visible branch of black feminist thought in direct opposition to an emerging sexuality studies. Jennifer Nash, in her essay "Strange Bedfellows: Black Feminism and Antipornography Feminism," goes so far as to say that "antipornography feminism's fingerprints smudge the lens through which black feminism examines sexuality, pornography and pleasure."[32] In viewing emerging black feminist debates on sexuality as promoting a kind of "sexual conservatism," Nash's critique falls squarely into the path of the problem I begin to outline here.

Lorde's "Uses of the Erotic," published in the same year as Gayle Rubin's groundbreaking "Thinking Sex," does the work of moving black feminist inquiry away from an understanding of *all* sexual minorities (perverts, prostitutes, pederasts, and sex workers) as having a *collective* stake in dismantling the regulatory regime of sex law.[33] In "Uses of the Erotic" emphasis is upon bridging the gap between *women* through deploying difference as a strategy of intersection rather than segregation.[34]

By seeing the erotic in opposition to a definition-lacking pornography, Lorde's essay secured her understanding of the line of demarcation between the two. This interpretation has its roots in an interview conducted in 1982 and published in the collection of essays entitled *Against Sadomasochism*. In this interview Lorde takes a stand against s&M practice by seeing it as part of women's experience of the pornographic and marshalling *a* black feminist thought against both the *kind of queer* subjects that Rubin would consider worthy of our attention and the type of *theorizing necessary* for such an engagement to take place. But in *Against Sadomasochism* it is not Lorde's interview that gives us a standard portrait of historical embeddedness because Lorde is careful not to subject her critique of s&M to a history specific to the black body. Instead, it is Alice Walker's epistolary engagement of the problem of s&M role play that calls attention to the problem of historical reenactment.

In "A Letter of the Times, or Should This Sado-Masochism Be Saved?," Walker recounts the following story: "Imagine our surprise therefore, when many of us watched a television special on sado-masochism that aired the night before our class ended, and the only interracial couple in it, lesbians, presented themselves as mistress and slave. The white woman, who did all the talking, was mistress (wearing a ring in the shape of a key and that she said fit the lock on the chain around the black woman's neck), and the black woman, who stood smiling and silent, was—the white woman said—her slave."[35]

Walker's "A Letter of the Times" reminds us that we can take history very personally, especially when the players line up so nicely. In the same volume, Judith Butler's "Lesbian s&m: The Politics of Dis-Illusion" (a piece originally written in 1980 during the period of her dissertation work) manages to strike the same spiritual high notes as Lorde's work does. As Butler writes: "Saying yes to lesbian sex seemed to mean saying no to heterosexist power. And it seemed to mean saying yes to a new and creative power. Opposing the notion of power as domination, lesbianism has meant for many of us a re-posing of power as the extension and creation of new ways of loving" (169). This kind of open-ended language by Butler certainly mirrors Lorde's sense of the expansive nature of women-loving-women community. At another moment during a critique of Pat Califia's call to prevent the policing of "our private fantasy lives" (171), Butler even goes so far as to say, "If I am trying to fight the Man and also worry about pleasing my sisters, I can see how private fantasy might become a haven of sorts. But the question is, is it a haven?" (172). Judith Butler—fighting "the Man"! Yet man or no man, the opposition between public and private here is still important in the early stages of queer theorizing—and I would maintain that this opposition has played a role in cementing what the objectives of an emerging discourse about "queer" would embrace.

In her final analysis Butler engages the "tension between moral feminists and sm." Like Rubin and Sedgwick, Butler would come to see feminist ethics as "moral" and therefore part of the regulatory regime of knowledge and power unduly directed at queer bodies that queer theory set itself up to thoroughly critique. Somewhere in this moral bathwater, the black female body swirls. Butler's claims in this early piece intersect with my work on desire because she is quick to remind us that "our desires are not so straight-forward. They are, I think, complexes of things, fears, hopes, memories, anticipations" (172–73). Ultimately she writes: "I am simply saying that to conceive of desire as a law unto itself [the sm position] . . . and the key to destroying repressive sexual orders is to exaggerate the autonomy and intelligence of desire." Here, Butler worries about the efficacy of desire as an end unto itself. Thinking through our historical location, Butler moves to drag desire through history's gantlet, reminding us that "there is no full-scale escape from our historical situation and the legacy of domination that has become ours" (173). In the end, Butler acknowledges that "it is crucial that both power and politics get reshaped and deepened from having passed through the lesbian experience. . . . There is also the 'power of the erotic' in Audre Lorde's essay of that name" (173). Walker, Lorde and Butler all rely upon some aspect of essentialist readings in order to make their collective point about power, women, and lesbians. I am most intrigued by Butler's use of the word "our" as a modifier for "historical situation," and I want this moment in her early work to return us to my recurring questioning of the matter of "history" among us. As we can see from the brief excerpts from all three critics, "history" means something very different for each of them. When Butler refers to history, she is absolved of having to specify its productive meanderings; when Walker speaks to history, she means ideologies of domination and subordination cemented during chattel slavery; and when Lorde nods toward the historical, she means the relationship between the state and the province of women's spiritual power. Here, history is capable of doing so many things to us and for us.

All of these definitional permutations are of some consequence to the landscape of queer theory as we know it. It is my contention that when we move toward the specificity of power, when we try to wrap our minds around it, we also begin to wrestle with the problematic attachments that feminists like Walker seem to give to those power relations.[36] Regrettably, whether Walker actually aligned "power" with the history of slavery or not, her use of the term would be taken as a direct reference to it, while Butler's use would appear universal, less particular, and therefore meaningful to everyone. Historical embeddedness reeks of insincerity when we allow blackness to take the burden of what should be political as personal. If we tie the black female body to the inevitability of slavery's abusive sexual terrain so that every time we think of enslaved black women and sex we think pain, not pleasure, then we also fail to acknowledge our own intellectual responsibility to take seriously how the transatlantic trade altered the very shape of sexuality in the Americas for everyone. To echo Spillers here, this is not a polite question to ask, but in my view a necessary one.

Against Sadomasochism includes the work of a diverse collection of women, many of them women of color. It is clear that Butler feels (at least in 1980) that she cannot have a discussion about desire or the erotic without directly engaging black feminist thought; years later she would be soundly condemned as having ignored it altogether. What happened to this moment of integration, this queer intellectual coupling? In what ways have we forgotten it while historicizing queer theory's rise from feminism in ways that make it easier to forget both this early crossing *and* profound disagreement? In many ways, Butler's later work continues to think through the impossible conundrum of having our cake and eating it too. How can desire's autonomy ever be fully expressed in a situationality that mires it in a *certain* history? How can we begin to speak to desire in productive ways without marking this history and making it matter? The question for my project is how can we mark and make this history without attaching it to some bodies rather than others? Ultimately, I argue, we have also lost the saliency of black feminist disagreement with an emerging queer studies project. In the next chapter I will demonstrate how that voice has been harnessed productively and nonproductively in intellectual interventions in the future of queer criticism. Recourse to history does not help to give clarity to our efforts to unseat biology, as quotidian narratives of black presence in the historical conjure a body wholly responsible for the history in which it is made manifest to us.

QUEER REPRODUCTION

Early practitioners of queer theory—many of them present at the important conference at Barnard in 1984 that resulted in the volume *Pleasure and Danger*—had to know about the back and forth between queer feminists and those aligned with Women Against Pornography. Women of color who did participate in the conference (Spillers, Moraga, and others) were wary of the move toward sexuality (and said as much in their creative and critical presentations), fearing that the problems of inclusion and voice that had plagued feminism would carry forward.[37] More importantly, the move toward queer theory and away from feminism cast feminist ethics as "moral" regulation and therefore jettisoned the ethical considerations upon which prevailing feminist criticism had relied.[38] It is important to note that Walker, Lorde, and Beauvoir are interested in how sexual practices relate to ongoing discussions of *feminist ethics*. I do not believe that these (black) prescriptive feminist concerns have translated into the less regulated environment in which queer studies finds itself. When queer of color critique performs the task of making black feminist and woman of color feminism matter to our theoretical projects, I do not know if *this* black feminist work on queer pleasure finds its way into the equation. In our subsequent understandings of what went wrong with queer theorizing, we somehow forgot the fact that *significant and visible* black feminists (Lorde and Collins, for example) absented themselves from a somewhat fruitful, if problematic debate about how we take our pleasure.

The result has had an equal and opposite effect. In some early queer theory, ethical or "moral" concerns would mire us in regulatory regimes that constrict the queer body as well as tether us to a stubbornly homophobic feminism; on the other hand, "ethical" concerns in late queer theorizing continually ensnare us in regimes of domination and suppression that mark the "ethical" as the place of whiteness and belonging in such words as "citizenship," "nation," and so on. What has been cast as ethical or moral is harassed by neoliberalism's long reach. What has been lost here is the desire to speak to the "ethical" in regard to the personal, since now it is perceived as being attached to a backward feminism or tethered to a corrupt ideology of global domination and biopower. Focusing on the personal in this formulation reduces the political impact of theoretical work by diminishing the importance of the state and its regulatory regimes. It is time to reassess what the personal is in the wake of history and how historical meaning is made in queer theorizing.

In essence, the debate about "sexuality" and black and colored bodies in feminist studies has yet to be concluded. Thinking through the very problem of s&m (in black and white) in the transition from one disciplinary home to another points to a possible wrinkle in the ongoing queer theory project. What is at stake in queer theorizing is to take this s&m scene and forget about its black/white casting, so that what queer theorizing says about *queer acts* (at least until queer of color critique) is wonderful so long as we do not get specific; so long as we do not get personal. In many ways, mainstream queer theory wants to leave history behind. I want to emphasize here that such desire is and can be fruitful, as the erotic scene can now move unencumbered by history's power play. What I want to argue with is the extent to which such a leave-taking does little to unpack the purposefulness of the black/white interaction in this *historical* scene. This purposefulness is one that marks our unwillingness to grapple with the binary, our adept reiteration of queer history's real trajectory, and our assignation of some histories to certain bodies.

I shall argue in the next chapter, perhaps very contrarily, that the personal is political, that absenting *these* somewhat conservative black feminist opinions from the women of color intellectual project performs damaging work. If we introduce the diversity of self-identified black lesbian feminist work to the conversation, will it mire us again in a historical repertoire that we find so annoying? Will S.H.E. (singular, historical, exogenous) prevent us from forgetting?

In truth, not even Cathy Cohen's intervention—which I discussed at length in chapter 1—could get queer *theory* to turn its head toward the political consequences of black.female.queer. And this is mostly because Cohen's overarching concern in "Punks, Bulldaggers, and Welfare Queens" is with queer politics, *not* theory. The political harasses the queer studies project that wants to envision itself as less *personal*, more global, and therefore of consequence. Nevertheless, Lorde's essay became a minor bump on the highway of high theory, and it provides one of the first black feminist injunctions against the messy contemplation of pleasure and desire that queer theory would undertake in the next two decades.

There have been sustained discussions and critiques of Lorde's work in black feminist criticism, and while much of it has been laudatory few have ventured to see the parallel between Beauvoir's design for the erotic and Lorde's conceptualization of its place in "women's" lives.[39] In the end, we seem to have accepted the abrogation here, so that the erotic appears to stand in fundamental opposition to, in Lorde's words, a "racist, patriarchal" society. I see in this subjection of "the erotic" to the sort of women's work that sits in opposition to the pornographic as both troublesome and somewhat undertheorized. Lorde boldly states: "The erotic functions . . . [as] a bridge between the sharers which can be the basis for understanding much of what is not shared between them, and lessens the threat of their difference."[40] The challenge is to address Lorde's *assumption* (and Butler's early though tacit adoption) of the view that the erotic "functions" as a means to undo difference, rather than facilitate its entrenchment.

On the other hand, what better way to understand racist practice than to gauge its particular investment in usurping the power of the erotic—the perfect location, according to Lorde, for the erosion of difference rather than for its reinscription. The erotic in queer hands works its magic because it functions in a very neat nonreproductive zone—it can be the repository of our desire for that nonreproductive ordering so necessary to a post-Edelman futurity, since "future" is already what comes after.[41] Even in Beauvoir's framework, there is space for the erotic to mean more to women than just a vestibule or passageway to the reproductive sphere. In many ways, the wrestling of the erotic from the zone of reproduction's inherent futurity has been a necessary move in feminist *and* queer scholarship, because it frees up the *gendered* body to do some extraordinary work.

I am not the first feminist scholar to point this out; Biddy Martin notes while reading Sedgwick that "gender, and the theory of gender offered by feminism, then, are associated with reproduction and with women."[42] Sexuality emerges and becomes recognized in the severance of the erotic from racist practice, from the pornographic, so that reproduction (the province of feminism) can be dispensed with and the act of forgetting what biology is for (racial belonging, procreating) can commence. Like Martin, I want to hold open the possibility of reproduction's meaning here—not for its relationship to women but rather for what its consistent practice says about the racial. Racist practice is still haunted by reproduction's persuasive arc insofar as the "racial" binds itself to the decision to pursue the future, the next generation. In order for queer studies to take this arc seriously, it must begin to see the *material function of the erotic*, and given the call for gay marriage and more reproductive and familial rights for queer subjects, its meaning in the *quotidian* course of queer life.

The problem that biology presented for feminism was worked out through the necessary sex/gender distinction in the late second wave. Once feminism understood biology (now not even "sex") to be as indeterminate as socially constructed sex roles (gender), then the category of "woman" could slip out from under biological necessity and societal baggage to roam freely with its "male" counterpart. Biddy Martin has pointed out the queer investment in the mobility of the male over and against the inflexible female quite articulately.[43] The importance of *overcoming* the "biological" in feminist discourse is evident in Sonia Kruks's review of Beauvoir scholarship, where she notes that "what these recent treatments of Beauvoir have in common is their return to her work as a site at which we may address impasses that confront feminist theory today. Taken together, they point us beyond unmitigated poststructuralism, toward a post-poststructuralism that reaffirms the importance for feminism of retrieving the lived experiences of embodiment and of overcoming not only biological but also discursive forms of reductionism."[44]

What I am arguing here is that race and racist practice mire an unfettered feminism in the materiality of the body and the idea of its limit. Where "the biological" is understood as "reductionism," the black racial project is excoriated for its crippling backwardness, since it is embedded in notions of the biological that do not help it make the case for better (racial) feeling. On the other hand, jettisoning the biological as the province of women in order to open up the space for queer (re)production does not facilitate the dismantling of racism's foundational logic. Queer theory's inheritance from feminism is, for many queer theorists, to continue to denounce talk of race as identity politics and ignore "racist practice" altogether, because these things are entirely disruptive to a theoretical project invested in the autonomy of (woman's) erotic preference, to echo Appiah. But, as postpositivist realist theory demonstrates, just because we eschew talk of race does not mean that racist effects vanish.

As materialist feminists raged against the poststructuralists and vice versa in the 1990s, it became clear that the *subject of woman* was not over just yet. While feminism might have conquered the biological determinism in which sex/gender was mired, it has yet to wage the battle against the same *biologism* embedded in the racist practice that produces race. A woman freed from her biology—whether through theory or technology, to remember Shulamith Firestone here—still faces the potential of that biology; its potential is written as a *racial* contract, to remember Mills here, as well as a gendered one.[45] When John D'Emilio proclaimed that "capitalism has led to the separation of sexuality from procreation," thus freeing "human sexual desire" from the reproductive sphere, he signaled the beginnings of a queer autonomy for the work of desire.[46] What he left behind is the ability of queer studies work adequately to account for racist practice in the midst of such autonomy. Perhaps this is the *ethical* moment that Beauvoir, Lorde, and Walker worry about? Racism turns us toward the *bare life* of procreation—regardless of how technology has freed us from the necessity of putting a penis in a vagina for procreative work to commence. We still have the messy nucleus of procreation's racial order to contend with—a racial order that in many ways is justified on both sides of the binary as either racial pride or nostalgic yearning.

While Beauvoir conceives of the erotic in often heteronormative terms, Lorde opens the door for its interpretation through diverse kinds of sexual configurations, which she explores more loosely in her biomythography, *Zami: A New Spelling of My Name.* In doing so, she comes dangerously close to the incest taboo—often a marker of absolute difference between subjects in the context of the family.[47] Judith Butler remarks on this particular prohibition: "What will the legacy of Oedipus be for those who are formed in . . . situations where positions are hardly clear, where the place of the father is dispersed, where the place of the mother is multiply occupied or displaced, where the symbolic in its stasis no longer holds?"[48]

Butler understands this challenge to the claims of social and cultural norms of kinship as the result of changing structures of relating among queer families (for lack of a better word). I offer that the question she asks can have more radical *claims* if she were to extend it to the infrastructure of American slavery—articulated as something imposed upon and practiced by us all, rather than something particular to certain bodies. Such claims to kinship—in black and white—were and are obliterated by liaisons created as a result of slavery's economic structure. Gone is the acknowledged relation among relatives; present is the raw nerve of the incest taboo, set aside for the purposes of securing national wealth and international dominance. The place of slavery in queer studies work has yet to be reckoned with, and this is perhaps because the boundary-breaking futurity in which queer studies finds its subject would balk if such a subject were held to a *transhistorical* vision of time—a vision that expands Foucault's conceptualization of a queer calendar to other historical events in its vicinity: a queer begetting of magnificent proportions![49]

Within five years of Lorde's *Sister Outsider* (1984), David Halperin helped to mark the trajectory of queer studies work with the following statement about sexuality as it was currently understood:

Sexuality defines itself as a separate, sexual domain within the larger field of human psychophysical nature. . . . *Sexuality effects the concep-*

tual demarcation and isolation of that domain from other areas of personal and social life that have traditionally cut across it. . . . Finally, sexuality generates sexual identity; it endows each of us with an individual sexual nature, with a personal essence defined (at least in part) in specifically sexual terms, it implies that human beings are individuated at the level of their sexuality, that they differ from one another in their sexuality and, indeed, belong to different types or kinds of being by virtue of their sexuality.[50]

By recognizing that sexuality must somehow be understood as something that represents a "demarcation," a cutting off from other "social life," Halperin pinpoints the problem embedded in early sexuality studies that still prevents us from thinking through race, sex, nation, queer in any way that can be agreed upon, *in practice*. For Halperin, the very modern idea of "sexuality" creates "the autonomy of sexuality as a separate sphere of existence." How did queer studies come to believe that sexuality holds the key to "the hermeneutics of the self"?[51] While it is not Halperin's project to spend time thinking through this question, it is clear in the critical race scholarship discussed earlier in this book that sexuality discovers its history during the rise of the age of reason. The taxonomy of post-Enlightenment life requires that we order sexuality and racial belonging. One can think of these movements as coterminous rather than separate and distinct. The biological determinism that made sexual acts mean something to male and female bodies came hand in hand with the kind of biological determinism necessary to make race(s) work.[52]

My reading of this coterminous becoming for race and sex would put Robyn Wiegman's work in conversation with Halperin's rather than relegate their contributions to two separate but important (if not equal) strains of critique. Race, sex, and sexuality might have emerged from the "New" World together, but it would be difficult to see them in the same room and consider their consanguineous condition outside of apocalyptic narratives that continue to order what racism, is, does, and means to us. As sexuality gained a hermeneutic that it could depend upon for evidentiary claims about *subjection* (not subjects), it pulled up and parallel to the bumper of race's fictitious known world.

Lorde is part of a long line of feminist "mothers" whose new age hopes for "women's" connection far exceeded their ability as women to practice what they preach. My goal in these pages has been to create an alternative genealogy for how the erotic became uncoupled from the arc of racism's reach. With this trajectory in mind, I now turn to queer critical attempts to bring race and racism back to the table of queer ideas. In the next chapter I focus on the discretionary claims of queer criticism's interdisciplinarity while simultaneously holding a brief for the loss and forgetting and unrecoverability of black.female.queer presence in the making of such critical interventions.

The deepest terror of every socially marked human being—
colored, female, queer . . . [is] that no matter what we write
think about or say, no matter how we fashion ourselves and
our work, we will be incessantly returned and reduced to this
single marking, that it will be produced again and again as
"the truth" of our being, our thinking, our worldly endeavors.
—Wendy Brown, "The Passion of Michel Foucault"

Those forced to wait or startled by violence, whose
activities do not show up on the official time line, whose
own time lines do not synchronize with it, are variously
and often simultaneously black, female, queer.
—Elizabeth Freeman, "Time Binds, or Erotohistoriography"

For even if I left, I would have to return, would have to recross
the borders of the United States, where the significance of
the "Negro" designation is so thoroughly sedimented that
it conditions even my attempt to forget what it means.
—Phillip Brian Harper, "The Evidence of Felt Intuition"

S.H.E.

Reproducing Discretion as the Better Part of (Queer) Valor

Colored. Female. Queer. Black. Female. Queer. The epigraphs above are ordered in a profound exceptionalism that convinces me that American studies did not have to go global to make the claim that the exceptional is certainly part of the rhetoric that glues understandings of who and what we are to one another. Black, female, colored, and queer share a simultaneity that opens them to violence, reduction, and forgetting. This is a historical ordering so sedimented, to echo Harper, that even our attempts to *forget* such a designation are futile. And we do want to forget, often in the very act of remembering. As Faulkner once offered, "memory believes before knowing remembers."[1] Black.Colored.Female.Queer. marks an undisciplined sector of the discipline: the representations of her have shifted from the dangerous and volatile to the abject and weak; S.H.E. (Singular. Historical. Exogenous) is both protector and protected. Her status continually reminds us that we have not yet accomplished our lofty goal of politically efficacious and practiced theory. In fact, *theory* fails her all the time. My goal in this chapter is to trace how we have simultaneously lost and found her (black, female, queer) in various critical attempts to have her mean something to the discipline of queer theorizing.

Wendy Brown in "The Passion of Michel Foucault" concludes her scathing critique of James Miller's homophobic assessment of Foucault with the epigraph I cite above. The arrangement she utilizes—"colored, female, queer"—is a common one, and since Kimberlé Crenshaw first coined the term "intersectionality" feminist critiques have been dogged by its absolute will to *discretion*—to represent each term in its discrete semantic location. For this particular critical conundrum, discretion is the better part of valor: it might be brave to think of these terms as intertwined, even messy, but it is much safer to chug along thinking of them as discrete, distinct, separate. But the categories "black," "colored," "female," "queer" point to a persistent problem in queer theorizing—how to have our queer theory and our feminism while still seeing the colored body or how to have our colored criticism while still seeing the female and the queer body and so on. My epigraph from Harper's work is meant as a playful rejoinder to the endpoint erected by Brown's grouping; we conclude with her, only to forget our entangled *relation*. The foregoing analysis suggested that queer studies needs critical race work in order to reassess its take on the erotic and in order for the antiracist endeavor to commence. This chapter chronicles the articulation of the queer studies project through various attempts (black queer studies and queer of color critique) to remind *it* of its persistent forgetting.

Although this mapping could have several origins, perhaps the best place to begin would be with the special issue of *differences*, "More Gender Trouble: Feminism Meets Queer Theory" (1994), in which several feminist theorists grapple with the "subjectless" critique of the new queer studies.[2] What is most obvious when reading "More Gender Trouble" is that there are more attempts here, in line with Eve Sedgwick's contribution to the field (*Epistemology of the Closet*), to commit finer acts of separation along the lines of Gayle Rubin's initial call to see sex and gender as separate. Elizabeth Weed, contributor and founding editor of *differences*, notes: "More accurately, the analytic space [Sedgwick] opens up looks to drive a wedge not simply between sexuality and gender, but between sex-sexuality and sex-gender."[3] In essence, the purpose of the collection is to speak for queer theory in a feminist context as well as to articulate which master narratives—deconstruction, psychoanalysis, knowledge-power—can and will be important to queer theory's painful but necessary final "break" from feminism, a break that Janet Halley attends to in her book *Split Decisions: Taking a Break from Feminism.*

But the *differences* volume (later published as a book edited by Weed) also arises at a particular moment in academic discourse. During its inception, "identity politics" was being soundly thrashed by those in the more theory-inclined Left who wanted to take a break from the noise being made by folks of color, to put it plainly. In Rosi Braidotti's conversation with Judith Butler about the shape of feminist theory in Europe, Butler remarks: "As you no doubt know, there has emerged an important and thoroughgoing critique of Eurocentrism within feminism and within cultural studies more generally right now. But I wonder whether this has culminated in an intellectual impasse such that a critical understanding of Europe, of the volatility of the very category, and of the notions of nation and citizenship in crisis there, have become difficult to address."[4] Butler's semantic trajectory here is telling and worth remarking upon in some depth.

She begins first by establishing a critical intimacy with Braidotti ("you no doubt know")—letting the reader also understand that this "thoroughgoing critique of Eurocentrism" is of some importance to their discussion. In the next step, she takes us right to what I call a *criticision*—somewhere between an intellectual statement and a bris—a critic's way of pronouncing the death knell for a particular intellectual line of inquiry by managing it like a nasty little killer T cell—excising doesn't always work, but it does produce a cleaner member, so to speak. Once the critique of "Eurocentrism" has been disarmed and appropriately managed then the efficacy of this critique is no longer certain. An important conversation within feminist and cultural studies (one that alludes to the rise of critical race discourse) is produced as an intellectual impasse—one that threatens the ability of "Europe" (the new subject here) to be able to speak its own diversity and destiny; one that includes the terms "nation" and "citizenship" rather than a term like "Eurocentrism." This effort to contain one term ("Eurocentrism") and redeploy others ("nation," "citizenship") is produced by a perceived "impasse." Since an impasse can be a dead end as well as a block to progress, Butler's language here reinterprets valid intellectual disagreement as dead end. Moreover, this impasse is also minimized to a misunderstanding of terms rather than a fundamental disagreement over the workings of racist practice. At this point in queer theorizing, the questions were never really about naming, although public debates devolved into the name game. Instead, what was at issue is, I shall argue, still at issue: to what *historical* trajectory would queerness attach itself, so that it could be legible to itself and to others? Which *geographic* locations would be meaningful for queer theory's central inquiries?

Butler has other reasons for casting a wide net over this embroiled debate. At the time, she was under fire in many feminist circles for being blind to race in general; a critique brought from the conference circuit to the publishing arena with Paula Moya's *Learning from Experience*.[5] In "More Gender Trouble," there is subtle if not detectable anxiety about the black body,[6] and it is clear that as the special issue moves from Butler's introduction to the interactive responses at the back of the volume, the more nuanced relations between "feminism" and its master narratives become, and the more we seem to lose the black body (critical or physical). This anxiety about the black (female) body and its function within queer studies work is evidenced in Evelynn Hammonds's "Black (W)holes and the Geometry of Black Female Sexuality" where she observes:

> I could perform that by now familiar act taken by black feminists and offer a critique of every white feminist for her failure to articulate a conception of a racialized sexuality. I could argue that while it has been acknowledged that race is not simply additive, or derivative of sexual difference, few white feminists have attempted to move beyond simply stating this point to describe the powerful effect that race has on the construction and representation of gender and sexuality. I could go further and note that even when race is mentioned it is a limited notion devoid of complexities. Sometimes it is reduced to biology and other times referred to as a social construction. Rarely is it *used* as a "global sign," a "metalanguage."[7]

Hammonds decisively points to the larger questions within queer studies work—questions that remain unanswered despite the emergence of black queer studies, queer of color critique, and most recently, the discourse of settler colonialism brought by native studies scholars.[8]

What to do with that black body that marks—at least in Hammonds's playful yet serious configuration—the *angry boundary* between feminism and queer studies by returning the fields to their cloying material life?[9] As if to answer this question in part, but in another vein, black queer studies inquiry stretches across two important publications: the special issue of *Callaloo*, "Plum Nelly: New Essays in Black Queer Studies," published in 2000 and edited by Jennifer DeVere Brody and Dwight A. McBride, and the volume *Black Queer Studies: A Critical Anthology*, edited by E. Patrick Johnson and Mae G. Henderson and published in 2005. In their introduction to "Plum Nelly," Brody and McBride ask "how might we conceive of the place of black queer studies?" (286). For both, that place or intellectual home is in African American studies, and their intent is to present the essays as a commentary upon that "home" and its lexicon rather than produce a sustained critique of queer studies and queer theory per se. "Plum Nelly" is important because it marks a serious departure from the politics of cultural specificity located in "identity difference" to what Marlon Ross in "Camping the Dirty Dozens" proposes as "identification as a temporal process" (291). This is a temporality that José Muñoz investigates as disidentification in his groundbreaking work *Disidentifications: Queers of Color and the Performance of Politics* and that Judith Halberstam later capitalizes upon in *In a Queer Time and Place: Transgender Bodies, Subcultural Lives*. As Ross notes: "Although it is impossible to 'evacuate' totally the grounding of cultural identity in spatial metaphor, we might be able to disrupt this spatializing tendency, at least temporarily, by thinking of cultural *identification* as a *temporal* process that enables and constrains subjectivity by offering up resources for affiliating with, while also disaffiliating against, particular social groupings, which themselves are constantly being revised over time by individuals' reconstitution of them" (291). Ross's critique is indebted to feminist theorizations about difference and is similar to the work of Muñoz, who explicitly borrows from this group's vocabulary to coin the term "identities-in-difference," which imagines that some "identities use and are the fruits of a practice of disidentificatory reception and performance."[10] The next generation of queer scholars of color would borrow from Muñoz the paradigmatic term "queer of color" and turn it into a critical critique, notably with the publication of Rod Ferguson's

Aberrations in Black and the special issue of *Social Text*, "What's Queer about Queer Studies Now?," edited by David Eng, Judith Halberstam, and José Esteban Muñoz. I will get to this new wave of queer scholarship at the end of this chapter.

Ross's lead essay in "Plum Nelly" focuses on black nationalist invective and its relationship to camp, and his argument is finely wrought, detailing the ways in which (black) nationalist critique has situated while also allowed for the presence of the black queer body. The battle that black queer studies wages here is one from within *and* without—one that mainstream queer studies and queer theory perhaps is free to disengage from. For white queer studies scholars to battle alongside queer allies in underrepresented groups the critique would get very messy indeed as white subjects—seen as always already privileged—would have to engage the particularized prejudice of marginalized peoples. In other words, is it possible for (white) queer theory to join in the call to interrogate the efficacy of black claims to difference?[11]

It is my contention that this somewhat thorny proposition—that white colleagues engage in the dismantling of African Americanist constructions of the black self—*keeps* black queer studies in particular from being embraced by both queer of color critique and other queer studies projects. The prohibition against calling out the disenfranchised (especially the black disenfranchised)—be they heterosexist or not—is still fully ingrained in neoliberal thought.[12] Nevertheless, as the movement for LGBTQ civil rights hits one roadblock after another, it is clear from the faculty meeting to the blog entry that white subjects *have* been more inclined to critique black subjects, even though such critiques are usually salted with the same kinds of bad analogy, historical sedimentation and outright racist invective that I have critiqued elsewhere in this project. But the forgetting of the black body—its relegation to *someplace else* in queer studies—continues, as there is something politically necessary that cannot be done, or even acknowledged as possible by (white) queer counterparts, without dire political consequences. The players here are disciplinarily defined (African American studies, queer studies) and the boundary between them makes a mockery of the very interdisciplinarity that critical mingling should foster. It seems that the racial divide haunts us continually, as we can still say, "you can say things that I cannot" and mean it with all sincerity. I am convinced that reimagining the erotic life of racism might hold some possibility for a critical *recuperation* here, as the focus on quotidian racist practice *and* its manifestation in the sphere of the erotic (who we love and how we *reproduce*) might disrupt our rather static notions of the black body and its historical repertoire (or the potentiality of its repertoire?) and the white critical body as it seeks to politely trespass upon it.

What we find in "Plum Nelly" is a subtle correction of the aesthetic and archival record that is queer theory, so that when Henderson ventures to mark Baldwin's *Giovanni's Room* as a metaphorical "closet," and then recalls his allusion to the "panic" incited by the homosexual, she can then remind Sedgwick that her reimaginings of the territory of the homosexual had in no small part been fully anticipated by Baldwin.[13] Again, we might ask ourselves why the African American (queer) canon is of little *theoretical* use to the (white) practitioners of an emergent queer theory. As with Butler's reading in *Bodies That Matter* of Nella Larsen's *Passing*, black example is mired in the biological—it is important when one wants to look at race meeting "queer" or some other category, but as Hammonds observes in the first incarnation of feminism meets queer studies: it is rarely used as a "global sign"—it always has *particularity*.[14] Examples of this theoretical tension abound in "Plum Nelly,"[15] and Michael Cobb's piece, "Insolent Racing, Rough Narrative," returns to the cadre of intellectuals in the Harlem Renaissance who contributed greatly to *queering* the very centeredness of race as a founding hermeneutic for an understanding of black being. What the black body is good for, at least theoretically, is wholly challenged not only in the primary texts of the Harlem Renaissance but also in the critical tradition that attempts to make sense of them. Why then this persistent need to see the black body as narrow referent, as reproducing a historical fixation for human being while simultaneously offering itself up to the *discipline* as someone else's to own and manage?

By the time queer studies evolves into queer of color critique in 2005, we are well on our way to the turn to the transnational in queer theory—a turn that inadvertently marks work that focuses on United States populations as problematically parochial.[16] What is interesting is that this turn is anticipated in "Plum Nelly" by Phillip Brian Harper's closing piece, " 'Take Me Home': Location, Identity, Transnational Exchange."[17] One could certainly argue that the first turn to the transnational comes out of Gloria Anzaldúa's very influential *Borderlands/La Frontera*—and this turn is in some part a response to how postcolonial criticism reconfigured the geographical reach of the transnational. Borderland theory pushed back on that remapping, thereby moving the intellectual fodder for discussions about racial difference to a psychic and material space that was more liminal and intimate; a space that ultimately privileged a principal hybrid subject.[18]

In recalling two experiences while in Canada—one with "trade" at a cash machine and the other at customs—Harper reflects: "If the discomfiture I experienced during my interview on the street is thus partly traceable to the anxiety with which I both recalled and anticipated my national-border crossing, then it would appear to constitute an instance—however paltry— of a particular psychic effect much commented upon in recent theoretical work. Specifically, it would seem to comprise the disorientation characterizing the *transnational imaginary* in the era of global capitalism."[19] I am reminded here of my discussion in chapter 2 of Sara Ahmed's attempt to use phenomenology's commitment to space and perception in order to think through what disorientation might mean to a queer project. Harper engages the "*transnational imaginary*" in an unraveling of his two experiences, which invoke problems of power, status, and ultimately conceptualizations of citizenship.

Toward the end of Harper's piece, he cautions against a move to the transnational as a corrective to the somewhat "limited" focus on issues affecting persons living within the United States. Instead, Harper suggests that the very same United States subject would find it hard to break away from this "inward orientation" even in their evaluation of all things *outward*. In closing, Harper suggests "that state-ideological functions can never be conceived apart from citizen-subjects whose activities and consciousness they call into being, which themselves certainly have not yet been unmoored from the imperatives of modern state nationalism."[20] Harper's analysis and caution has great usefulness for this study, as it redirects our attention to the potential for subjects traditionally marked as "among the oppressed" to inhabit a certain kind of privilege—the erotic life of racism rears its ugly head—while also indicating a moment in (black) queer theorizing where the turn to the transnational is perceived as risky, if not intellectually suspect. Harper worries that our attempts to look "outward" do not always compel us to think that our own actions and reactions are part of the problem that we seek to engage; this doubling back upon the self—a kind of critical self-reflection—is crucial to the work of theory. But what happens to these critical maneuvers in the next incarnation of the empire strikes back for black queer studies?[21]

For Johnson and Henderson in *Black Queer Studies* the goal is to "reanimate" African American studies and queer studies so that African American studies can take into account (again, now the second call) the importance of sexuality (not just hetero) to its intellectual project and so that queer studies can find a way back to thinking about the take on race by African American studies in that project. Although Johnson and Henderson do not allude in their introduction to the "Plum Nelly" collection, they seem to set for themselves a similar trajectory. But the increasing anxiety about the particularity of the black body is evident in their introduction:

> In its current configuration, the volume's content is clearly centered within the regional context of the United States. Nonetheless, we are aware of the very important implications of diaspora and postcolonial studies relative to black American sexuality. We are also conscious of the sometimes narcissistic and insular theorizing of U.S.-based academics who do not thoroughly engage the impact of globalization and U.S. imperialism on the transnational flows of racialized sexuality. . . . Our focus here primarily on U.S. racialized sexual politics is not meant to be totalizing or polemic but rather strategic. Black queer studies is a nascent field and we feel compelled to prioritize a concomitant *embryonic* theoretical discussion within U.S. borders in order to make an intervention "at home," as it were.[22]

Johnson and Henderson unwittingly reinscribe the particularity of blackness and its specificity—its "embryonic" nature—in order to make a brief for attention to its geographic and historical situationality.

I cannot help but comment upon the use of the terms "embryonic" and "nascent" to describe a black queer studies project. These words testify to the important status that reproductive metaphors have for work on race. While the heteronormative properties of reproduction appear to be what "queer" stands in opposition to, how can such metaphors be useful to a black queer studies manifesto? The literary critic in me wants to hold a brief for the (shadow) importance of reproduction here because it sutures race to the erotic. When one makes an argument for a "racial" project, the terrain turns rocky very quickly because one is now obliged to do a certain kind of race work, and this work, erotic or otherwise, enlists racist practice. The real time of reproduction's orthodoxy—biology/race—creates the conditions under which black queer studies can now become visible.

As if in anticipation of this problem, Johnson and Henderson also acknowledge the critique of their position offered by one of the essays in the collection, Rinaldo Walcott's "Outside in Black Studies: Reading from a Queer Place in the Diaspora." In this essay Walcott asks, "Why is it that the black studies project has hung its hat so lovingly on U.S. blackness and therefore a 'neat' national project? And how does a renewed interest in questions of the diaspora seem to only be able to tolerate U.S. blackness and British blackness?"[23] While Johnson and Henderson seem to deflect the transnational moment by addressing it in the introduction, there is the nagging sense that a project on United States blackness marks it as parochial, a claim made by some critical race scholars in their attempt to unwed racist practice from a black/white paradigm mired in a specific geographical space. It has been my contention throughout this study that this black/white binary is constitutive of the racial imaginary, since so many evidentiary claims about racist practice return repeatedly to this specter of absolute difference. It is time to bring our imaginary in line with our critical practice—it is time to come clean about the erotic charge of racist endeavor. One way to begin this work is to rethink the place of reproduction (not as hetero or homo, not as feminist or women's) and its attention to biology, race, and belonging.

Once the authors have outlined the province of black queer studies, they then direct their attention to an overwhelmingly "white" queer theory. As E. Patrick Johnson reminds us, "*there is some 'race' trouble here with queer theory.* More particularly, in its 'race for theory,' queer theory has often failed to address the material realities of gays and lesbians of color."[24] Here again a black (racial) project is set in opposition to a white (racial) project, so that the black/white binary is wielded to do some heavy lifting, while the editors make the simultaneous claim that black queer (racial) belonging is a different kind of project altogether. Similarly, in "Beyond the Closet as Raceless Paradigm" Marlon Ross, citing Maurice Wallace's contribution to the dismantling of "the closet" as a particularly "gay" metaphor, and continuing a critique embedded in Henderson's take on Baldwin in "Plum Nelly," argues: "(white) queer theory and history are beset by what I call 'claustrophilia,' a fixation on the closet function as the grounding principle for sexual experience, knowledge, and politics, and that this claustrophilic fixation effectively diminishes and disables the full engagement with potential insights from race theory and class analysis."[25] In arguing that the closet metaphor helps to link the coming homosexual community to a "powerful narrative of progress," Ross also notes that the very genesis of queer critique—Foucault's knowledge-power theory—relies upon an erasure of the racialized body (read by Ross as "black," not white) in order to prepare it for its inscription as homosexual. In his analysis, the work of the sexologists casts reproduction for the homosexual as a failed function of *and* a failure to reproduce the Anglo-Saxon.

This brief emphasis on the importance of reproduction to the invention of the homosexual is of great consequence for this study because it marks a crucial point at which the two branches of queer studies I have been following here *both* repudiate the reproductive for *homosexuality* and banish it from the theoretical center of queer discourse. I have argued earlier that this movement away from reproduction's material force also had much to do with queer theory's need to take a break, echoing Halley, from feminism. In Ross's redaction of the sexologist's findings, the failure to (re)produce the Anglo-Saxon is part of the constellation of lack in which the very idea of the homosexual rests. If we were to take reproduction here as part of the matrix of racialized desire, we can then see how this turn away from reproduction is racially marked, not because it reveals a loss of Anglo-Saxon sanguinity per se, but because it also produces reproduction as a function of white racial belonging rather than as a function of all racial belonging.

In light of my musings about reproduction and feminism in chapter 2 I want to engage two arcs of thought in queer studies engagements: one in which reproduction (a feminist province) is utilized as a failure of whiteness, and the other in which this failure is coded as always already a property of one racial group over another where the concern is for white racial reproduction, not black racial reproduction. The particular embeddedness of desire (the erotic) and racist practice—both of which come out of the defining of reproduction here—is hard to see. Every time we say queer theory and think or feel an opposition between black and white, the erotic shadow of racist practice casts itself on the wall. Queer studies takes the high road by continuing to view its racial inheritance as something to be repudiated (a repudiation that I read in Miss Rosa's rejection of Sutpen's proposal in *Absalom, Absalom!* in the conclusion to this book); a repudiation manifested in its focus on the biopower of the child. This repudiation is often celebrated as something queer theory can be proud of. But this renunciation also comes at a cost, as it places blackness outside of the lifework of reproduction, thus losing the material function of blackness in the discourse of reproduction *and* homosexuality, as well as its culpability —its ability to serve as an agent and actor—in the quest for racial belonging. Although I have taken issue with the way in which "white" queer theory is deployed here, Ross's critique serves to dismantle many of the assumptions of universality and collectivity embedded in the word "homosexual."

In picking up on the challenge to (white) queer studies posed by black queer studies scholars, queer of color critique emerged between *Callaloo*'s "Plum Nelly" and *Black Queer Studies* with the publication of Roderick Ferguson's *Aberrations in Black* (2003), a book that grounds the discussion of queer theory in the work and contributions of "women of color."[26] Ferguson's redaction of women of color feminism observes that "it attempted to negate the normalization of heteropatriarchal culture and agency by the inchoate global economy. Indeed, black lesbian articulations of difference, queer identity, and coalition bear traces of this negation" (118). In his introduction to the book he announces that "queer of color analysis presumes that liberal ideology occludes the intersecting saliency of race, gender, sexuality and class in forming social practices," while also noting that it "extends woman of color feminism by investigating how intersecting racial, gender, and sexual practices antagonize and/or conspire with the normative investments of nation-states and capital" (4). Given my earlier explication of some black feminist investments in the discourse on sexuality, it is clear that these "normative investments" litter black feminist thought, making "liberal ideology" the possession of whom and for what ends? In essence, Ferguson's question and my own would be: do all of black feminist critics necessarily stand outside of "liberal ideology?"

In sum, this is a tall order for black feminism in particular, as its particular theoretical might is figuratively used to usher in a queer critique that focuses upon "historical materialism." For Ferguson, "put simply, women of color feminism, generally, and black lesbian feminism, particularly, attempted to place culture on a different path and establish avenues alternative to the ones paved by forms of nationalism" (118–19).[27] The slippage between women of color and "black" is neatly negotiated by Ferguson—this is a welcome addition to feminist thought—but my query here has to do with what kind of work the category "woman of color" both recognizes and obfuscates. With such heavy emphasis upon dismantling the status quo at the intersectional thoroughfare, black feminism must be represented as an *exceptional* entity, capable of sitting in the vanguard of sexual liberation.

There are familiar elements here—the importance of intersectionality, for one—but there is also new territory, as Ferguson follows Muñoz's lead in identifying what role "queer of color" can play in critiquing global capitalism and normative heteropatriarchy.[28] In addition, there is a profound shift not only in the underpinnings of the queer theory project, but also in the bodies that such a project might take as its imaginary/imagined focus. By changing the arc of queer theory's citational terrain, Ferguson moves away from the genealogy that extends from Foucault outward, to one that might begin with Marcuse and Davis, and extend to Lowe, Sanchez, Hong, Goldberg, Mercer, and Sandoval, to name a few. In queer of color critique, gone is the citational repertoire (e.g., Butler, Sedgwick, Halperin, Warner) found in both black queer studies projects. This reordering is a profound shift in queer theory, and my attempt here is both to laud this bibliographical shift and also to think through what Ferguson is asking of us as theoretical practitioners. In essence, what does queer of color critique want us to do, really?

What comes out of this evolving critique is the way in which the black (female) body as the vanguard theory of a woman of color feminism again signals the intersection, or to borrow words from Hortense Spillers, is "vestibular to culture."[29] Can a body of work be a new paradigm? My query leads me back to Hammonds's desire to have race be a "global sign," rather than something to be remarked upon perfunctorily so as to get it out of the way. Now that S.H.E. is in the center, will the landscape of queer theorizing shift to acknowledge her presence?

Nevertheless, Ferguson's contribution does build upon critical race work in that he is attuned to racist practice. He notes by way of Chandan Reddy's work that "racist practice articulates itself generally as gender and sexual regulation, and that gender and sexual differences variegate racial formations. This articulation, moreover, accounts for the social formations that compose liberal capitalism" (3). By focusing on racist practice *as* gender and sexual regulation Ferguson provides a useful paradigm, as do his colleagues in black queer studies, for our understanding of racist practice.[30] I take this notion a step further by returning the focus on the regulation of sexual practices to the terrain of reproduction—where racist and homophobic practice cohere for nation-state and neighbor.

It is clear that in focusing upon queer of color critique *and* global capitalism, scholars like Ferguson (and by extension Muñoz and Reddy) want to return the saliency of "woman of color feminism" to ongoing materialist debates about sexuality in the age of transnational flows. As Muñoz writes in *Disidentifications*, "If queer discourse is to supersede the limits of feminism, it must be able to calculate multiple antagonisms that index issues of class, gender, and race, as well as sexuality" (22). By this time in the theoretical game, feminism has solidified as a project that should be superseded, which gives it the status of a relic and simultaneously excises the very contributions of women of color to the production of a very diverse feminist discourse that queer of color critique is poised to commit itself to. The difficulty lies in this deployment of black.female.queer as an entity whose historical underpinnings necessitate a situation where S.H.E. (Singular, Historical, Exogenous) is functionally illiterate, where S.H.E. can be forgotten, and where her intellectual contributions matter insofar as they awaken the senses to a past politico-knowledge formation in which S.H.E. can be readily contained. Her figuration at this point in our critical history looks profoundly like that of the native subject in Phil Deloria's *Playing Indian*, where ideas of nation, place, and origin are wholly invested in seeing and believing in the archaic native—in promoting a dead zone (think "impasse")—one echoed here by the figuration of black.female.queer.

Can the aims of the "woman of color" feminist project be harnessed for discussions about liberalism in a post-9/11 world? Before I answer this question, it is important to note that I am naturally suspicious of the terms "liberal" and "liberalism," which queer of color critique attempts to turn our attention toward in the next iteration of the critical project. The work of liberalism marks the political landscape around us so severely as to sever one population from another so that liberals are out there somewhere and the rest of us (call us black feminists) are wedded to the always already political critique or rigorous action. But, as we all know, any marriage provides safe harbor for infidelity. Critiques that cannot seem to bear the weight of their own conclusions—ones that segregate as well as discriminate—worry me to no end and open themselves up for a profound skepticism, if not devastating blindness for this black.female.queer. What kind of legibility will a black.female.queer *critique* have if she falls outside of the neat political boundaries set for her in the roll call of critical agents?

I am not the only queer theorist who has had difficulty with liberalism's significance to the queer studies project. In *Terrorist Assemblages: Homonationalism in Queer Times*, Jasbir Puar notes that "it is precisely by denying culpability or assuming that one is not implicated in violent relations toward others, that one is outside of them, that violence can be perpetuated. Violence, especially of the liberal varieties, is often most easily perpetuated in the spaces and places where its possibility is unequivocally denounced. . . . It is easy, albeit painful, to point to the conservative elements of any political formation; it is less easy, and perhaps much more painful, to point to ourselves as accomplices of certain normativizing violences."[31] Puar's insistence that "normalizing violences" can proliferate, even in critical work is crucial to my project. In the end, I ask: what more normativizing act can there be than to participate in *reproduction*? And given its normativity, a classification that we are indebted to queer studies for illuminating, what kinds of work within the racial project does reproduction perform?

As if in answer to this question, David Eng, Judith Halberstam, and José Esteban Muñoz—the editors of the special issue of *Social Text* "What's Queer about Queer Studies Now?"—assembled to query the "political utility of queer" by imagining "a renewed queer studies ever vigilant to the fact that sexuality is intersectional, not extraneous to other modes of difference, and calibrated to a firm understanding of queer as a political metaphor without a fixed referent" (1). Their words here are clearly poised to take on the challenge issued in David Halperin's early essay ("Is There a

History of Sexuality?") to think through the way in which sexuality became unhinged from other social and political practices.

Given the events after 9/11, the editors of "What's Queer about Queer Studies Now?" find a certain historical and political urgency for a new queer critique—one that makes the turn to the transnational a *fait accompli*, as "queer diasporas" problematize "what could be called queer liberalism" (1).[32] Queer liberalism is not only a province of whiteness, it is also deeply invested in the export of American ideals and ideas that might not be transferable to a larger world order. The veiled critique here concerns itself with "whiteness" and also, implicitly, with the kind of parochialism observed in United States critical practices. This queer liberalism has also been remarked upon in the work of M. Jacqui Alexander, who observes that "an early epistemic marriage between queer theorizing and the dominant methodologies of poststructuralism in the U.S. academy has had the effect of constructing queer theory in a way that eviscerates histories of colonialism and racial formation."[33] Liberalism, especially queer liberalism, pointedly disregards "histories of colonialism and racial formation"—a liberalism that queer of color critique utilizes woman of color feminism to stave off. Alexander rehearses the feminist argument that poststructuralist accountings of quotidian life fall short of the mark in recognizing the complexities of intersectional existence, yet the "subjectless" critique has such provocative pull on the queer imaginary that its intellectual claim of doing certain work for us is prima facie and seductive. The editors of "What's Queer about Queer Studies Now?" see the potential for a radical break with queer liberalism while concomitantly investing in a notion of queer as a political though unfixed referent. Can such high hopes for queer's flexibility be able to contain the twenty-first-century contours of black.female.queer?

When the editors cite the recent and "significant body of work on theories of race," however, they do not mention a single book by queer studies scholars who also happen to identify as black, female, and lesbian, although their work can be recognized under the moniker, woman of color feminism.[34] In addition, while they acknowledge the importance of nation, state, governmentality, and sovereignty, they miss an opportunity to engage a host of Native American studies scholars and their founding presence in debates both here and abroad on the capricious nature of such terms. To point this out in the special issue of *Social Text* is to think through my own intellectual work as a queer studies scholar, as the move away from the messiness of identity politics toward something that looked more fluid and inclusive almost necessitates a forgetting, a leaving behind of the parochial, often represented by black.female.queer. In essence, when queer theory looks outward, to remember Harper's caution, it often engages in the particular "American" practice of forgetting black.female.queer. If she appears at all, she is reproduced within the confines of a delimiting (historical) racial practice, one for which we can have no accounting.

To bring us back to that body is a risky move indeed, but my attempt here is not only to make that move but also to understand it as a move toward the relational, rather than the singular. Therefore, the "body" that I seek here has a very *queer* materiality, for it is simultaneously forever absent and always already present—we can always marvel at its ability to matter so much, and then not matter at all. Black being is deeply invested in whiteness, to the extent to which racist practice dictates how they and we belong to one another. My attempt here is not to throw shade on an extraordinary collection or to belittle the place of queer of color critique in the queer theory project. Rather, my questions point toward the larger issue of *losing a queer black body*. Citing black.female.queer in queer theory is a forgetting that has proportionate outcome across sexuality studies. Black.female.queer voices are foundational, but not generative, as there is little active engagement with the diversity of this relational voice. It is my contention that the overarching problem here is that queer of color critique is not solely addressing the remnants of identity politics, but the object of queer theory's ongoing ridicule: a feminism that somehow turned the corner on the black body and never looked back. Underneath the critique of queer liberalism is actually an argument about feminist claims upon both the black body and its historical specificity.

The editors of "What's Queer about Queer Studies Now?" acknowledge both the efficacy of " 'queer of color' critique" and the extent to which such critique might contribute to what they call "queer intersectionality" (6). While earlier projects like "Plum Nelly" and *Black Queer Studies* see critical race theory as a fruitful genesis, queer studies now embraces the critique within critical race theory of a "U.S. nation-state"–based "conceptual frame" as parochial, thus bringing to fruition the fear by black queer studies that lack of attention to a "diaspora" abroad might eventually hurt its inquiry. But the idea of the nation-state as United States based elides the possibility that native governments exist in contested relationship with this nation-state, often unmarking and remaking its boundaries and turning the idea of "abroad" into home once again. It seems here that the queer reiteration of the "subjectless" critique produces material effects—too high to get over, too low to get under. In wanting to preserve some of the poststructuralist pie—a move that Alexander warns is difficult to sustain— "What's Queer about Queer Studies Now?" has to jettison something.

The issue's lead essay, "Punk'd Theory" by Tavia Nyong'o, engages the work of Cathy Cohen and, by extension, the problem of "intersection"; and even in its concluding moment, it riffs off of the work of Ann duCille in heralding the intersection as a dangerous place.[35] Racial blackness and vernacular culture are at the heart of Nyong'o's piece, and it is clear from the start that queer of color critique's most valuable contribution to queer studies work is the relentless interrogation of this thing called "queer theory." Joon Oluchi Lee reminds us: "While queer theory has made tremendous efforts to interweave the political discourses of race, class, and gender in the theorization of queer identification, it is rarely the case that such 'generous' theoretical gestures actually make it out of the box into the practiced lives of sexualities and genders." In the same breath Lee also aligns feminism with a problem particular to gay male theorizing: fear of the moniker "female." He declares: "Gay male critics fear 'female' and in this they have an ally in second-wave feminism—because the work of gender identification is ultimately seen as a system of impermeable biological boundaries, whose operation is totalizingly hierarchical."[36] Again, the specter of the biological appears at the precise moment feminism is called to account, and Lee is quick to note that the refusal of the "female" position is problematic for a queer (male) theory inherited from feminism. What is problematic here is that Lee claims for "feminism" a totalizing perspective that is not supported by feminist critical attention to this issue. There was and still is a debate within feminism about the problem of the biological— a problem that has been reinterpreted as "white" feminism's claim on a particular racial order. But this idea of "feminism" would have to separate woman of color feminism from the larger and therefore *real* feminist project, an exclusion that I have maintained elsewhere is more practiced critique than actual archival truth.[37]

Amy Villarejo's "Tarrying with the Normative" on black history takes the challenge posited in Ferguson's book—to bring race and class (through Marxist analysis) to queer theory's table—as foundational to her own method. Villarejo is right about Ferguson's inheritance from British cultural studies, and hers is the only sustained critique of Ferguson's claims in the collection of essays. Within that critique, Villarejo acknowledges Ferguson's fusion of "feminist critique with queer critique," a recognition of alignment that deserves some scrutiny here, as the "feminist" project is taken by Villarejo and Ferguson to now be about "heteropatriarchy." The major step forward here seems to be the privileging of a woman of color feminism within and as feminism. Villarejo's quarrel with Ferguson stems from his deployment of the term "nonheteronormative" to both designate "a pathologizing racial logic" and "figure of defiance and critique" and from his treatment of sociology and literature as canonical equivalencies (72, 74). Her argument with Ferguson's use of "nonheteronormative" as a both/and proposition cuts across the particular problem of citing black.female.queer in queer studies projects. The both/and position is not only hard to sustain, but also unwieldy.

In Villarejo's text, "African American" is often seen side by side with "exploitation, degradation, abjection, and exploitation" (73). Villarejo astutely marks the place where "African American" becomes too high to get over and too low to get under in the rhetorics of racist practice through which the term comes to be *known* by each and every one of us. "African American" is both a sign of contestation (revolution?) and exploitation. This problematic relationship to blackness returns me to Harper's remarks in the epigraph to this chapter that even our attempts to escape such structured definition rely so heavily upon it that we inevitably must treat the encounter as an act of profound and *impossible* circumnavigation.

Villarejo then proceeds to propose a counterreading by thinking through Ferguson's missed opportunity in regard to the "critical potency of queer theory. . . . [which] offers ways to fly with language and desire away from homology and continuity. . . . [It] can offer . . . a way to grapple with feeling and with response (affect), a way to work in the interstices of contacts, affiliations, relations" (75). In essence, Villarejo wants to preserve for queer of color critique the importance of queer theory's openness to feeling and affect. Because Villarejo's critique is centered upon a sustained reading of Ferguson's contribution to the field and his readings of literature, she does not have room to deploy other queer African Americanist readings of black "literature." A host of black queer studies work on the place of the literary in black culture cannot be engaged here, and so there is a missed opportunity to document, at least via footnote, all of the dissenting queer black voices in this call to think through the place of the black literary imaginary in the queer of color critique project.[38] This is the moment in Villarejo's essay where a nod to the black studies project would create connection, if not relationship, between the two subfields.

I would like to propose that the call to revere "women of color feminism" also serves to mask its historical specificity as well as contribute to its unmaking. The work of "intersectionality" as it is marked in the essays in "What's Queer about Queer Studies Now?" serves as an interesting case in point. The boldest challenge to "intersectionality"—which always already has its foundational trace in Crenshaw's early work and has been construed since then, thanks to Patricia Hill Collins, as a black feminist theoretical apparatus—is expressed in Jasbir Puar's essay, "Queer Times, Queer Assemblages." She writes:

> The Deleuzian assemblage, as a series of dispersed but mutually implicated networks, draws together enunciation and dissolution, causality and effect. As opposed to an intersectional model of identity, which presumes components—race, class, gender, sexuality, nation, age, religion—are separable analytics and can be thus disassembled, an assemblage is more attuned to interwoven forces that merge and dissipate time, space, and body against linearity, coherency, and permanency. Intersectionality demands the knowing, naming and thus stabilizing of identity across space and time, generating narratives of progress that deny the fictive and performative of identification. . . . As a tool of diversity management, and a mantra of liberal multiculturalism, intersectionality colludes with the disciplinary apparatus of the state. (127–28)

Having said all of this, Puar then cautions us with a footnote: "This is not to disavow or minimize the important interventions that intersectional theorizing makes possible and continues to stage, or the *feminist* critical spaces that give rise to intersectional analyses" (138; emphasis mine). I have practiced a similar caveat at the start of my critique of queer critique; such premonitory statements indicate the presence of an unsettling anxiety. There are two gestures at work in this disclaimer: that the important interventions of intersectionality are known because they are unnamed, and that "intersectional analyses" are the particular property of feminism. Interestingly enough, several black feminists, chief among them Cathy Cohen, have already argued intersectionality's narrowness, so why the anxiety about minimizing a critique that has already been under intense scrutiny? That Puar's assessment of *intersectionality's* feminist appropriation reads as its mandate is troubling; that she anticipates the critique is seriously smart.

In reading this collection of essays one witnesses the contemporary playing field for black.female.queer narrowed considerably: these bodies have resonance *historically*, but they do not figure as *contemporary interlocutors* to engage, debate, or theorize around. The trans black prostitute that conjures up the tale of queer of color critique in Ferguson's first iteration is indeed vestibular to culture: she is Vanna White turning the letters so you can see them and hopefully get paid. My argument here is not that black.female.queer critics have *not* been solicited for inclusion in the *Social Text* special issue; rather, my critique seeks to get beyond the exclusion/inclusion problematic that has dogged much of contemporary theorizing. My comments here are meant to engage the *conditions* under which something called black-queer-feminism (woman of color feminism) *can* be engaged. These conditions mandate a forgetting that is temporary but nonetheless quotidian (insofar as the repetition of such an exclusion is played out).

Gayatri Gopinath is another contributor to the special issue of *Social Text* who acknowledges the contributions of critical race theory, specifically the work of Stuart Hall, but the critical race citation here focuses on the conceptualization of diaspora from Hall rather than the United States–based critique grounded in an interrogation of everyday racism. When the queer meets diaspora in Gopinath's "Bollywood Spectacles," it enables and "becomes a way to challenge nationalist ideologies by insisting on the impure, inauthentic, nonreproductive potential of the notion of diaspora." The "nonreproductive" gets requalified as "domestic space outside a logic of blood, purity, authenticity, and patrilineal descent" (158). While these are laudable aims for a queer project, they do point toward the particular ways in which queer endeavors are marked by a compulsive theoretical privileging of the nonreproductive. As I have argued throughout this book, why should we assume that a queer (non)reproductive space is outside the bounds of racist practice? Moreover, given that queer families abound, why is "queer" marked as nonreproductive?

But in Gopinath's essay we do find a further articulation of Ferguson's project as she reminds us that queer of color critique is poised "to reject the parochialism of American studies as well as the underlying heteronormativity of even its postnationalist versions" (159). The black queer studies concern about its own parochialism is echoed in Gopinath's assessment of what queer of color critique can and will do, but the door opens, at least citationally, on a conversation with these scholars about the place of populations at home in relationship to the overwhelming "heteronormativity" of the American studies project. Black queer studies has had much to say about this problem and the expectation should be that a conversation ensues; instead, this discourse falls between the cracks of a narrowly defined American studies and a retooling of the postnationalist space as heteronormative. In the *Social Text* collection we are ever reminded of the importance of "diaspora" as a critical move outward. This also leaves a native studies critic like myself wondering what to do with issues of native sovereignty and presence within the tightly construed matrix of United States–based versus diasporic critical engagements. One could certainly find fodder for a queer studies project in the fact that the only queer marriage in all of Oklahoma that was actually legal occurred under the auspices of the Cherokee nation. But how would a black queer studies or queer of color critique project open itself to a discussion of this queer romance if it is blind to the ways in which native peoples have also shaped discourse about the diasporic as well as the national, both at home and abroad? Even in the context of calling for renewed respect for contributions by women of color to discourses about sexuality and nation, the different parts of a new queer studies project are not speaking to one another.

Toward the end of the *Social Text* collection, Michael Cobb assesses the intersection of race, religion, hate, and incest and observes that "blackness should not [be] merely testimony or autobiography. Blackness, instead, functions most effectively as a powerful language of critique."[39] This pull to the universality of (black) critique is definitely evident in the special issue and it reminds me of Hammonds's call to see race (read black) as a "global sign." But the call to think about "blackness as a powerful language of critique" *produces* a unity of vision within black intellectual work that is difficult to sustain. Moreover, in heralding our ability to see past the autobiographical moment, we forget how importantly those quotidian experiences shape the diversity of black being. In calling for more attention to the quotidian *materiality* of critical hubris, I attempt in this book to think through how this loss of black biodiversity becomes evidence of an unsettling critical anxiety.

Cobb's essay is one of the few in the collection, let alone in queer theory, to utilize the theoretical contributions of Hortense Spillers. I would like to take a moment by way of conclusion to return to one of her most influential pieces, "Mama's Baby, Papa's Maybe," which was written in 1987. In one pivotal moment in this essay, Spillers ventures to offer the following: "Indeed, we could go so far as to entertain the very real possibility that 'sexuality,' as a term of implied relationship and desire, is dubiously appropriate, manageable, or accurate to any of the familial arrangements under a system of enslavement, from the master's family to the captive enclave. Under these arrangements, the customary lexis of sexuality, including 're-production,' 'motherhood,' 'pleasure,' and 'desire' are thrown into unrelieved crisis" (231). Spillers boldly suggests that sexuality's very vocabulary has been altered by human being's bizarre machinations under slavery. Cobb is right to ascertain that scholars need to return to Spillers's work and its applicability to sexuality studies. If these categories—motherhood, pleasure, desire, reproduction—in sexuality's abridged dictionary are thrown into crisis by the institution of slavery, where does that leave the overall study of sexuality? Notice here that Spillers does not offer a prescriptive analysis of the meaning of reproduction, motherhood, pleasure, or desire for black bodies; instead her critique hinges on a variety of pressures that slavery exerts upon all manner of human relation. Hammonds returns to the spirit of Spillers's foundational piece when she remarks upon the "global sign" that race refuses to become in feminist and queer theorizing.

Spillers's observations also point toward a very important dialectic in the erotic life of slavery: that the conditions of contact imply "non-freedom for both or either of the parties" and have reverberations "from the master's family to the captive enclave." Slavery's influential arc, captured in Spillers's pointedly grotesque arc of flesh separated from the body of the enslaved by the master or overseer's whip, touches and irrevocably alters the dynamic between white and black bodies. My only slight correction here is in the relative distance Spillers maintains between "master's family" and "captive enclave," thus reproducing the idea that law and practice somehow cohere in the slaveocracy. But it is the lie of difference between us—"master's family" and "captive enclave"—that makes what matters in slavery of biological concern, thus making its repercussions and erotic life pertinent only to black life. In historical references to the importance of blackness to queer studies, this same separation between black and white is maintained, so that even when we marshal the history of colonialism and slavery for use in our analyses, these histories seem to be useful or only have meaning to black subjects.

Does black femaleness carry the sign of history's reach upon us so completely that we must give her up in order to go about our theoretical business? Having jettisoned "reproduction" for heteronormativity, and having assigned black.female.queer a very high critical standard to live up to, the ability to speak to her quotidian messiness has been lost altogether. In Janet Halley's mixed assessment of the question with which I began this section on queer studies work—what is the relationship between feminism and queer studies?—there is some consideration of the problem. In *Split Decisions: How and Why to Take a Break from Feminism* (2006), Halley spends a good portion of her time redacting key feminist arguments, intersecting them with one another and with theoretical paradigms from queer studies. She states, "I argue here for a politics *of* theoretic incommensurability" (3). By constituting queer theory as a "break" from feminism—one that she encourages—Halley has the inconvenient task of determining which arguments are most representative for both accounts. While I am all for a move toward agreeing to disagree in critical discourse, I am less enthusiastic about the methodology Halley employs to move us in this direction.

In the sub-section of part 2 of *Split Decisions* "Convergentist and Divergentist Hybrid Feminism" Halley utilizes the Combahee River Collective Statement as a black feminist contribution to mainstream feminist theory. When she compares it to Mackinnon and Spivak, the (w)holes are evident and one wonders why she chose a political manifesto instead of a piece of (black) feminist theory for her comparison. Why mix genres here? In essence, why not use Spillers, for example, or Mae Henderson? I am not trying to say that the collective and its statement has had little significance in feminist theorizing; what I am arguing for here is more attention (again) to the diversity of opinion among (black) feminists as well as some attention to the *political differences* that genre demands and marks for scholars.

But the observation above is both beside the point and part of my larger one as well: the diversity of voices of black feminist theorists cannot be taken into account because if they were the theoretical landscape would be altered to such a great extent that the queer project Halley envisions would find itself in "unrelieved crisis," to echo Spillers. Halley's redactions of pivotal critical stances within feminism and queer theory constantly urge us to think differently about what feminist theorizing is asking us to do (for women). In preparing scholars of sexuality studies to take a break from feminism, she considers what feminism asks of us by producing a series of lists as a rhetorical measure. The first list—gleaned from Adrienne Rich's famous list in "Compulsory Heterosexuality and Lesbian Existence" —is produced with the following caveat: "Do you like the ur-list of structuralist feminism? Or does it make you feel paralyzed? Take your time; really read it slowly; read it the way you would a poem by Gertrude Stein" (195).[40] In this list the characteristics of male power are enumerated:

1) *To deny women* [our own] *sexuality* [by means of clitoridectomy and infibulations; chastity belts; punishment, including death, for lesbian sexuality; psychoanalytic denial of the clitoris; strictures against masturbation; denial of maternal and postmenopausual sensuality; unnecessary hysterectomy; pseudolesbian images in media and literature; closing of archives and destruction of documents relating to lesbian existence];

2) *Or to force it* [male sexuality] *upon them* [by means of rape (including marital rape) wife beating; father-daughter, brother-sister incest; the socialization of women to feel that male sexual "drive" amounts to a right; idealization of heterosexual romance in art, literature, media, advertising, etc., child marriage; arranged marriage; prostitution; the harem; psychoanalytic doctrines of frid-

gidity and vaginal orgasm; pornographic depictions of women responding pleasurably to sexual violence and humiliation (a subliminal message being that sadistic heterosexuality is more "normal" than sensuality between women)];

3) *To command or exploit their labor to control their produce* [by means of the institutions of marriage and motherhood as unpaid production; the horizontal segregation of women in paid employment; the decoy of the upwardly mobile token woman; male control of abortion, contraception, childbirth; enforced sterilization; pimping; female infanticide, which robs mothers of daughters and contributes to the generalized devaluation of women];

4) *To control or rob them of their children* [by means of father-right and "legal kidnapping"; enforced sterilization; systematized infanticide; seizure of children from lesbian mothers by the courts; the malpractice of male obstetrics; use of the mother as "token torturer" in genital mutilation or in binding the daughter's feet (or mind) to fit her for marriage];

5) *To confine them physically and prevent their movement* [by means of rape as terrorism, keeping women off the streets; purdah; footbinding; atrophying of women's athletic capabilities; haut couture, "feminine" dress codes; the veil, sexual harassment on the streets; horizontal segregation of women in employment; prescriptions for "full-time" mothering; enforced economic dependence of wives];

6) *To use them as objects in male transactions* [use of women as "gifts"; bride-price; pimping; arranged marriage; use of women as entertainers to facilitate male deals, e.g., wife-hostess, cocktail waitress required to dress for male sexual titillation, call girls, "bunnies," geisha, *kisaeng* prostitutes, secretaries];

7) *To cramp their creativeness* [witch persecutions against midwives and female healers as pogrom against independent, "unassimilated" women; definition of male pursuits as more valuable than female within any culture, so that cultural values become embodiment of male subjectivity; restriction of female self-fulfillment to marriage and motherhood; sexual exploitation of women by male artists and teachers; the social and economic disruption of women's creative aspirations; erasure of female tradition]; and

8) *To withhold from them large areas of the society's knowledge and cultural attainments* [by means of noneducation of females (60% of the world's illiterates are women); the "Great Silence" regarding women and particularly lesbian existence in history and culture; sex-role stereotyping which deflects women from science, technology, and other "masculine" pursuits; male social/professional bonding which excludes women; discrimination against women in the professions]. (195–97)

I reproduce the "ur-list" in its entirety to demonstrate its specific purchase, not only upon Halley's envisioning of early queer feminism's assessment of women's situation, to echo Beauvoir, but also upon our own conceptualizations of when and where black.female.queer enters into the historical arc of feminist theorizing. This list could easily serve as a manifesto for the antislavery society, where the ways in which "[slaveholding and nonslaveholding] men" exert control over enslaved women seem very similar, but not one of the examples of male power includes the range of possibilities for the enslaved person, or mentions "slavery" as a constitutive practice of "male power." I am not trying to argue that "slavery" *should* automatically be associated with black.female.queer; instead, what I want to point out here is the way in which this particular epoch in United States history is easily elided in both Rich's and Halley's schema. It is a forgetting that recalls the thorny place of the black female body in feminist accountings of itself. It is as if the history of slavery literally belongs to someone else—it is another *disciplinary* terrain. Having fashioned this history as the property and responsibility of the subaltern others in United States culture, the project of feminist theorizing and, subsequently, queer theorizing can commence.

Black.female.queer occurs in Halley's reiterative enumeration as if it were contained in psychic brackets; brackets made even more seductive by Halley's insistence that we read the "ur-list" as if it were "a poem by Gertrude Stein." Later in her reading of how to take a break from feminism, Halley finds a way to reproduce Butler's earlier attempt to make sense of "Eurocentrism" and the culture wars. By yoking black feminism to a morally bankrupt and outmoded "convergence feminism," Halley can then package "it" in her later "thought experiment" as an impossible apparatus for achieving (feminist) justice in legal jurisprudence. In a case involving pregnant women at the workplace, she concludes: "Convergentist feminist antiracism and feminist postcolonial work seek solutions that *merge* the interests of black workers, offshore workers, and pregnant women in the United States. And I agree that it is very important to seek possibilities of such merger, and to act on them politically. But even to see them clearly you have to be willing to see moments in which their interests don't converge, and you have to be ready to decide when to give up and do things for one group of workers at the expense of another" (288). I am inclined to agree with her that at least in legal practice some interests will be accommodated over others. At the end of the last piece in her examination of specific legal cases, Halley can confidently assert: "One motive force driving the Brain Drain [in feminist scholarship] is, surely, the ferocious preclusion imposed on inquisitive minds and avid justice seekers by a paranoid structuralist and prescriptive convergentists presuppositions, indeed by the stricture that *theory must create living space*" (341; emphasis mine).

I must be honest and say that while reading Halley's brilliant take on several complex and vexing legal decisions involving sex, gender, and sexuality, I am in agreement with her about the legal and theoretical stakes of narrow (feminist) approaches to them. What I find here, however, is that the way in which Halley *parses* that theoretical universe does nothing (1) to represent the diversity of the black feminist position she then repudiates; (2) to challenge the foregoing (lesbian) feminist claim to women's particular situation; or (3) to address the ways in which the jettisoning of black.female.queer is a foundational turn in queer theorizing. What Halley has *not* taken a break from is feminist theory's deployment of the black body and its insistent, even cloying material recall.

Social Text's "What's Queer about Queer Studies Now?" along with queer of color critique seek to redress this particular "wrong" in queer theorizing by centering their critique upon foundational texts in women of color feminism—a feminism that has its grounding in black feminist work. Caught in the middle between the struggle to forget and to remember, S.H.E. stands wholly outside or in vestibular relation to feminism and queer theory, respectively. "Aragorn, it is you who are now responsible for middle earth."

If we exclude all references to slavery's economies of reproduction and desire, then we can make very discretionary claims about its influence upon us, while simultaneously forgetting the (black and white, brown and red) bodies attached to its sorrow and woe. If we attach these bodies to a thoroughgoing feminist catalogue of degradation at the hands of men, then we will not be able to speak to the forgetting that must take place in order for queer theory (or feminist theory) to commence, because wouldn't such a momentary lapse in responsibility, if not manners, warrant the full force of angry black feminist response? It is my contention that we must break the cycle of our critical attachments by breaking with the tradition of producing black.female.(queer) in a historical register that matters only to her. By breaking with this mode of inquiry, we might be able to reach an epiphany of sorts—one that would allow us to see what happened to us *collectively*. This collectivity might restore just what we did and do to one another at the moment of our intimate interactions—erotic, racist, and otherwise. This is the erotic life of racism that this book endeavors to unveil. It is the last repository and also perhaps the first of our affective desire(s).

Much of this book has focused upon theoretical work in order to make its larger point. In the conclusion I shift registers to examine the "touch" as a metaphor for both our erotic commitments and our "biological" relations in the context of a literary reading. In the course of this examination, I think through Derrida's explication of the touch and utilize this framing for a reading of what is generally thought to be an American classic about race, caste, and gender: Faulkner's *Absalom, Absalom!* In sum, I tentatively seek to answer one of the most thoroughgoing speculations of this project: what kind of readings would we create, if the lie of nonrelation was and is not available to us?

Conclusion
Racism's Last Word

This concluding chapter is an experimental exploration of the intimacy upon which *everyday* racism relies. The work here is not focused upon egregious or spectacular acts of racist violence, but instead investigates the more quotidian acts of racism—the kind that separate (and simultaneously conjoin) black and white in family genealogies, the sort created by a simple touch or a word uttered between "blood strangers," a term I deploy in the introduction to mark both the saliency of race as a trope and the absurdness of race as an ideology. In order to do this work, I deploy a series of scenarios, passages, and scenes to mine the connection between race and gender *and* what we understand as the experience—the feeling—of racism.

The first section, "The Last Word," reads Derrida's provocative essay "Racism's Last Word" and Toni Morrison's musings on the same subject in order to explore the role of language in our understandings of how racism is articulated. The second section, "Faulkner's Touching Moment," provides a reading of Rosa Coldfield's narrative in William Faulkner's novel *Absalom, Absalom!* that complicates the question of the touch. Throughout this reading, touch appears as an appropriate metanarrative for racism because it engenders outrage *as well as* identifies connection in past, present, and future. The attempt is to read racism through gendered and raced examples of its triumph. The touch, I suggest, manifests itself as the psychic life of difference, transforming two categories of being (human and nonhuman) into a charged space of pleasure *and* of possibility. The third section serves as a bridge between explications of Faulkner's novel, using the controversy over Thomas Jefferson's heirs and their final resting place to ask questions about the practice of slavery and its psychic life. The fourth section returns to *Absalom* and provides a reading of the category "human" in Rosa Coldfield's refusal of Thomas Sutpen's marriage proposal.

THE LAST WORD

As I have argued earlier, in order to talk about race we need to understand its connection to racism. Such an exploration is even more necessary in an environment where our desire for color blindness has made it possible to separate race from racism, its constant companion. Critical musings about the end of race or about the inadequacies of the category altogether have assumed that race pilots itself through national narratives, fictional enterprises, or family albums. This is not the case. Even as we pronounce the death of race, we cannot overlook the fact that our attempts to articulate it into oblivion, to pronounce the last word on race, simply have not worked.[1] In keeping with the speculative nature of this chapter, I want to shift here to a metaphoric rendering of "the last word" in order to meditate upon our *simultaneous* search for the end of race and our strivings for an adequate articulation of it. An apt example of this arduous quest is Toni Morrison's selection of the final word of her great novel *Beloved*. In her essay "Home," published after the novel, she discusses its ending: "Someone saw the last sentence of *Beloved* as it was originally written. In fact, it was the penultimate sentence if one thinks of the last word in the book . . . as the very last sentence. In any case the phrase, 'Certainly no clamor for a kiss,' which appears in the printed book, is not the one with which I had originally closed the book."[2]

Upon her editor's suggestion, Morrison looked for a word that was not so "dramatic" or "theatrical" as the original, now erased ending. She continues:

> I was eager to find a satisfactory replacement, because the point that gripped me was that even if the word I had chosen was the absolute right one, something was wrong with it if it called attention to itself— awkwardly, inappropriately—and did not complete the meaning of the text, but dislodged it. It wasn't a question of simply substituting one word for another that meant the same thing. . . . I am still unhappy about it because "kiss" works at a level a bit too shallow. It searches for and locates a quality or element of the novel that was not, and is not, its primary feature. The driving force of the narrative is not love, or the fulfillment of physical desire. The action is driven by necessity, something that precedes love, follows love, shapes it, and to which love is subservient. In this case the necessity was for connection, acknowledgment, paying-out of homage still due. "Kiss" clouds that point. (6–7)

In closing her remarks on writing *Beloved*, Morrison adds: "My efforts were to carve away the accretions of deceit, blindness, ignorance, paralysis, and sheer malevolence embedded in raced language so that other kinds of perception were not only available, but were inevitable. That is the work I thought my original last word accomplished; then I became convinced that it did not, and now am sorry I made the change. The trouble it takes to find just one word and know that it is that note and no other that would do is an extraordinary battle" (7).

The right word can also bring "the acknowledgment" that puts the erotic life of the text in motion, a place in *Beloved* where categories of difference can also be at play. Morrison has not revealed what that word might be, but I can't help but think that the original "last word" hovers somewhere between "fuck" and "touch." Regardless, Morrison documents the quest for the penultimate pronouncement on race—if one can think of the novel as a relentless meditation upon slavery's racist brutalities—as ultimately unfruitful. Nevertheless, she does capture the inadequacy of the word "kiss" to an articulation of fraught and dangerous relations between white and black subjects under slavery's racist imperative. Morrison's struggle with the word "kiss" and her attempts to work around "raced language" points to the complex nature of racism and our attempts as writers and critics to write a narrative of its permutations. Her reliance upon and repudiation of the erotic life of racism indicates that we do find racism in the arena where intimates make "connection."

The French philosopher Jacques Derrida also attempts to explore "the last word" in his essay from 1985 "Racism's Last Word," which is more aptly translated from the French as "The Last Word on Racism."[3] Derrida, however, deploys the metaphor in a different fashion. Speaking of the word "apartheid," he notes that the word remains the same no matter what the natural language in which it is embedded. He observes that "no tongue has ever translated this name—as if all the languages of the world were defending themselves, shutting their mouths against a sinister incorporation of the thing by means of the word, as if all tongues were refusing to give an equivalent, refusing to let themselves be contaminated through the contagious *hospitality* of the word-for-word" (331; emphasis mine). Derrida uncannily uses a tongue/turn similar to that employed by Zora Neale Hurston in *Their Eyes Were Watching God* (1937). Janie, the primary protagonist, pronounces: "Mah tongue is in mah friend's mouth." Feminist and African Americanist critics have consumed reams of white paper devising intricate and seductive theories about this statement. Surely one is that the phrase, "Mah tongue is in mah friend's mouth," is both a figure of speech and an erotic declaration; its mimetic qualities abound. If we take the tongue, we must also accept the word—"the contagious hospitality of the word-for-word"—where Hurston troubles Derrida.

In general, many of Derrida's critics often take exception to his focus upon the play of language, rather than upon the more concrete nature of material conditions.[4] I would argue that Derrida's language play opens up new possibilities for our understanding of racism and its legacy of action. In addition, his vision of racism points to our inability to own it; to see it as a possibility for past, present, and future. In working with the tongue and the word or, more precisely, with the simultaneity of repudiation and acceptance that so characterizes racism's contradictory terrain, Derrida highlights the active nature of racism:

> At every point, like all racisms, it [apartheid] tends to pass segregation off as natural—and as the very law of the origin. Such is the monstros-

ity of this political idiom. Surely, an idiom should never incline toward racism. It often does, however, and this is not altogether fortuitous: there's no racism without a language. The point is not that acts of racial violence are only words but rather that they have to have a word. Even though it offers the excuse of blood, color, birth—or rather, because it uses this naturalist and sometimes creationist discourse—racism. . . . institutes, declares, writes, inscribes, prescribes. A system of marks, it outlines space in order to assign forced residence or to close off borders. It does not discern, it discriminates. (331)

Like Hurston, Derrida envisions tongues exchanging. His concept of "contagious hospitality" underscores the problem of treating the tongue as a contaminant, insisting that the inevitable exchange (commingling) is dangerous; that the act of transference and translation itself is corrupt.[5] The hospitality he refers to here is often interpreted as from outside—and the implication is that apartheid therefore comes from some "foreign" place—that the word is not given to us by our "friends." Thus "hospitality" is a contagion, making the wor(l)d a dangerous place. Perhaps the most pernicious aspect of any sustained conflict between peoples is that phrases like "separate but equal," "the final solution," and "apartheid" are not the creations of institutions, of governing bodies, and of our enemies. They are also the inventions of our intimates, our friends, our neighbors, and our blood relations. Remember the transatlantic slave trade, Indian removal, and the Holocaust; witness Algeria in the 1950s; Bosnia in the 1990s—the list is endless. Friendship is often the first "gift" of war.

The trope of the tongue works in two directions: we engage in a word for word, tongue for tongue reciprocation or we perform a refusal through abstraction—refusing to incorporate the word in our own lexicon (making word and deed an aberration), rejecting it as someone else's experience (racism is for or happens to one group over another), someone else's language (the word does not befit the deed, the act), and ultimately, someone else's problem. And the problem of racism is always someone else's to own—it has a place in that it occurs at the level of the everyday, but it does not have a home—it manifests, but only as a fantastic event—an aberration in an otherwise lovely day. Its exceptionality is its beauty. If the word does not have a place (no origin, no nation), a point of passing and passage (two tongues intertwined), it ceases to exist.

In his essay "Le Toucher: Touch/To Touch Him," Jacques Derrida expounds upon the myriad objectives and complicated interactivity of the touch: "For to touch, so one believes, is touching what one touches, to let oneself be touched by the touched, by the touch of the thing, whether objective or not, or by the flesh that one touches and that then becomes touching as well as touched. This is not true for all the other senses: one may, to be sure, let oneself be 'touched' as well by what one hears or sees, but not necessarily heard or seen by what one hears and sees, whence the initial privilege of what is called touch" (136). Though touching a person may seem simple, it is anything but. Both physical and psychic, touch is an act that can embody multiple, conflicting agendas.[6] It can be both a troubled and troublesome component in the relationship between intimates, as in the case of Derrida; or, alternatively, the touch mediates relations between friends and strangers.[7] In fact, the touch can alter the very idea as well as the actuality of relationships, morphing friends into enemies and strangers into intimates. For touch can encompass empathy as well as violation, passivity as well as active aggression. It can be safely dangerous, or dangerously safe. It also carries a message about the immediate present, the possible future, and the problematic past. Finally, touch crosses boundaries, in fact and imagination.[8]

Ironically, even though we shrink from our experience of quotidian racism, we are apparently incapable of living without categories of difference, even when those categories are at worse hurtful and at best fictions in and of themselves. My central questions here are as follows: "What makes difference work?" and "How do we accomplish its goals?" I again come back to racism as the action that makes race matter. In a psychoanalytic register, Freud offers an account of our need to differentiate. He surmises that "even where the original inclination to identification has withstood criticism—that is, when the 'others' are our fellow men—the assumption of a consciousness in them rests upon an inference and cannot share the immediate certainty which we have of our own consciousness."[9] In other words, even when we recognize someone as "human," we destroy the pleasure of recognition and of reciprocity. We do not permit ourselves fully to interpret or see the human we encounter as having the same consciousness or even the *potential* for the same as us. While my purpose here is not to engage Freud's complex deliberation(s) about the human psyche, it is noteworthy that the work of difference, as conceived of by Freud and perhaps as experienced by all of us to some extent, is never really complete. Our desire for absolute difference cannot be satiated. It keeps coming back to question the legitimacy of our own claim that we really are a single and unique consciousness. There is no endpoint to our gambits with the other, which breaks in upon our singularity, causing us to react indignantly, "Oh, it's *you* again?" We feel the same burden when touched by another. The touch, crossing boundaries, affirms the inadequacy of this boundary between selves.

The power of the touch as both boundary and trespass is wonderfully illustrated in the following explication of one of William Faulkner's greatest novels. In one now (in)famous scene in *Absalom, Absalom!*, Rosa Coldfield exhibits hysterical rage when Clytie (Sutpen's "half black" daughter) arrests her ascent of the staircase at Sutpen's Hundred by placing a hand upon her arm. Behind this gesture and the anger it provokes is a terrible story. For Faulkner's most famous novel is organized around a family saga that takes place in the old and the new South and extends beyond the Civil War. In 1833, Thomas Sutpen arrives in the town of Jefferson, Mississippi, with a "design" to build a mansion and establish a hundred-acre plantation: "I had a design. To accomplish it I should require money, a house, a plantation, slaves, a family—incidentally, of course, a wife. I set out to acquire these, asking no favor of any man" (218). Shortly afterward, in 1838, he marries Rosa Coldfield's older sister Ellen. As the novel takes several temporal and narrative shifts, we hear the convoluted tale of Sutpen's early years. Before his arrival in Mississippi, Sutpen's first attempt at fulfilling his design goes awry when he discovers that the woman he marries in Haiti is not white but Creole. He puts her aside in New Orleans and travels to Mississippi. But his design is again challenged when his son from this first union, Charles Bon, plans to marry his half-sister, Sutpen's daughter and Rosa's niece, Judith. Charles Bon is literally the past coming back to haunt Sutpen's design. In order to prevent the marriage, Henry Sutpen (son of Judith and Thomas) kills Charles and then disappears. Henry's reasons for committing murder are always a matter of speculation throughout the text.

In the novel's present tense (January 1910), the narrative is pieced together as Quentin Compson and Shreve Davenport sit in their Harvard dormitory recalling the story as told to Quentin by Rosa and his father, Colonel Compson. Rosa's first-person narrative, contained in chapter 5 of *Absalom, Absalom!* encompasses both her return to Sutpen's Hundred just after Henry Sutpen kills Charles Bon and the seven-month period when Rosa, Clytie, and Judith wait for Thomas Sutpen to return after the Civil War. When she arrives at the foot of the stairs in 1864, within two years of Ellen's death, Henry Sutpen has killed Charles Bon and vanished; Judith, Bon's intended, stands outside the door she will not open, clutching her wedding dress in one hand and the picture of Charles's New Orleans wife (like father, like son) in the other. Clytie stands between Rosa and the door beyond which the dead body of Bon resides.

In this signal passage, we find Rosa obsessed with Clytie's "black arresting and untimorous hand on my white woman's flesh" (115). Listen to Rosa's rage, which exemplifies my concept of "the touch":

> Then she touched me, and then I did stop dead. Possibly even then my body did not stop, since I seemed to be aware of it thrusting blindly still against the solid yet imponderable weight . . . of that will to bar me from the stairs; possibly the sound of the other voice, the single word spoken from the stair-head above us, had already broken and parted us before it (my body) had even paused. I do not know. I know only that my entire being seemed to run at blind full tilt into something monstrous and immobile, with a shocking impact too soon and too quick to be mere amazement and outrage. . . . Because there is something in the touch of flesh with flesh which abrogates, cuts sharp and straight across the devious intricate channels of decorous ordering, which enemies as well as lovers know because it makes them both. . . . But let flesh touch with flesh, and watch the fall of all the eggshell shibboleth of caste and color too. Yes, I stopped dead—no woman's hand, no negro's hand, but bitted bridle-curb to check and guide the furious and unbending will—I crying not to her, to it; speaking to it through the negro, the woman, only because of the shock which was not yet outrage because it would be terror soon, expecting and receiving no answer because we both knew it was not to her I spoke: 'Take your hand off me, nigger!' (115)

What makes Rosa's obsession with Clytie's touch so remarkable is that even in the midst of absolute chaos and trauma, Rosa chooses to focus upon that touch and its possibility. Here, the touch assumes experiential knowledge, while it also calls upon its witnesses and players to testify to it as connection and repudiation, making it part of that person's experience and daring her to dis-own it. The parallels to Derrida's conceptualization of nations refusing an intimate exchange—"word-for-word" refusal—are several and uncanny. When Rosa finally utters the word "nigger" at the end of this rambling scene, it is almost anticlimactic; she has already proven that the touch does transform, or at least it has the possibility to translate, to convey meaning from one to another. The touch is vividly personified and, as an entity in the text it is always already present—it does not happen to Rosa so much as it *connects* Rosa and Clytie in a past whose imbrication occurs through blood and law. Rosa and Clytie become, literally, *blood strangers*. Like Derrida's conceit about racism's incorporation and repudiation by national bodies, Rosa's narrative refuses the touch at the same time that it proves its inevitability throughout time, rather than in time. In essence, the touch transforms, becomes legible because it moves beyond "the negro" and becomes "it"; Rosa begins to see the touch as her adversary ("I crying not to her, to it; speaking to it through the negro, the woman") and as she realizes this, she also embraces its unequivocal presence.

Faulkner renders the touch between Clytie and Rosa as not solely violent, but erotic. The touch is so compelling here that the prevailing narrative of race is undone and a multitude of possibilities find fruition. The language of the passage is entirely visceral—as Rosa's body moves forward within the action of the novel, her mind is arrested and preoccupied with the inevitability of the touch. The mind/body split that Rosa endures mimics the structure of racism—how everyday people play the game of distancing themselves from racism by seeing it as not part of their daily routine but as someone else's devastating failure at communication. She runs headlong into the "truth" of the past—her blood relationship to Sutpen's black and white family—that renders the language of getting there absolutely inarticulate. Language is literally "broken"—ungendered and unraced. It hovers in chapter 5 of *Absalom, Absalom!*, witnessing its own demise as there is no adequate language for Rosa's experience of Clytie's touch, which is why we have such a convoluted articulation of this moment by Rosa. The touch they share potentially unmakes gender, as it dismantles racial difference because the two women are called upon (through Rosa's voice) to contemplate the meaning of difference, to reside in the space where a gendered connection is made (im)possible by racism's quotidian assault. Rosa's panic is made all the more inviting because of Clytie's relative silence—a silence that Faulkner makes very few attempts to move beyond.

In another manifestation of difference, Rosa remarks: "Even as a child, I would not even play with the same objects which she [Clytie] and Judith played with, as though that warped and Spartan solitude which I called my childhood . . . had also taught me not only to instinctively fear her and what she was, but to shun the very objects which she had touched" (116). Faulkner identifies Rosa's personification of "objects" as they become intermediaries between one body and another. Rosa's "objects" *are* constitutive of "the human." How we become "human" then is mediated by an ever-present "touch" of the material, the object, the not-us, threatening incorporation. Moreover, what Rosa reacts to is not the threat of belonging to (sharing the same gene pool with) Judith and Clytie; she later says that she sees them as no different than she. Rather, Rosa's reaction to Clytie's touch introduces the threat of belonging. But the anxiety caused by this threat is only perceived—it is only a performance, if you will, because each character in *Absalom, Absalom!* fully understands that the commingling which she or he loathes has already taken place. The "objects" at work in the book take on the position of the virtual body, representing both "terror" and "pleasure" and eliciting a simultaneous response from the reader —titillating fear and absolute disavowal.[10]

The intimate moment that Rosa and Clytie share is ordinary. It is quotidian intimacy that forces us to realize the other as some*one* with whom we interact and have an impact upon; our acknowledgment of this connection represents the touch and its fruition. We do not create intimacy; it is there awaiting our recognition.[11] Let me rephrase this: we are bound intimately to others whether we realize or acknowledge such connection. The touch is the sign without a language to make it legible to "others." Rosa's experience of Clytie's touch creates a psychic presence so powerful that it draws another woman, Judith Sutpen, into its web. In the end, the women—Rosa, Clytie, and Judith, like the three Fates—become "one being" (129). For Faulkner, the touch "abrogates." It nullifies our stubborn insistence upon separation between races, sexes, or nations, if you will. After all, in Faulkner's "modernism," black and white bodies do not always occupy separate spheres. What is at stake here is not presence at all, but the idea of it; the knowledge, no matter how circumscribed that "presence" is only (as with Clytie) half the story.[12]

JEFFERSON'S GRAVE DISTURBANCE

In spring 2001, NPR's *Morning Edition* ran a report about the Thomas Jefferson Heritage Organization and its attempt to preserve the "character" and "reputation" of our third president. The organization had produced a six-hundred-page report stating that the DNA evidence linking Jefferson to Sally Hemings's children was inconclusive. John Work, an eighth-generation relative of Jefferson and president of the Thomas Jefferson Heritage Society, was "deeply disturbed by the thought that President Jefferson slept with a young slave."[13] What astounds me is that the relatives who champion Jefferson do not see the fact that he owned slaves in the new republic as any kind of stain on his "character" or "reputation." Jefferson's detractors see the connection to Hemings as evidence of the "complicated" nature of early American society. His advocates see this "evidence" as a complete occlusion of what it means to be a "founding father" in the first place. What is in jeopardy is (white) paternity.

In addition to this report, NPR also ran a story on Alice Randall's novel *The Wind Done Gone*, a parody of Margaret Mitchell's *Gone With the Wind* told as a series of diary entries by the illegitimate and enslaved half-sister of Scarlett O'Hara. In its first attempt, the Mitchell estate successfully sued to stop the initial publication of Randall's parody, citing violation of copyright law by infringing upon the estate's sequel rights. The decision was eventually overturned in appellate court, and *The Wind Done Gone* eventually reached the public. Cheryl Crowley of NPR interviewed several writers and critics about the book, one of whom was Lauren Berlant of the University of Chicago. All of them noted the dominance of the now infamous classic, how its "mythic portrayal of the South" is more widely read and available than histories of "plantation life" and "reconstruction." In addition, Berlant, speaking for the academy, argued that the novel has achieved a kind of "normative" status in the imagination, providing a cultural fantasy that endures.[14] Even Jefferson's own words cannot curb our lust for the fantasy of slavery—its "human" refuse, if "refuse" here denotes both "trash" and "renunciation." In speaking about our nation's "manners" in *Notes on the State of Virginia*, Jefferson remarks:

> There must doubtless be an unhappy influence on the manners of our people produced by the existence of slavery among us. The whole commerce between master and slave is a perpetual exercise of the most boisterous passions, the most unremitting despotism on the one part, and degrading submissions on the other. Our children see this, and learn to imitate it; for man is an imitative animal. This quality is the germ of education in him. . . . The parent storms, the child looks on, catches the lineaments of wrath, puts on the same airs in the circle of smaller slaves, gives a loose to his worst of passions, and thus nursed, educated and daily exercised in tyranny, cannot but be stamped by it with odious peculiarities. The man must be a prodigy who can retain his manners and morals undepraved by such circumstances. (168)

We are left to wonder if Jefferson is that prodigy and, therefore, exception to the will to tyranny. If the root of the word "prodigy" vacillates between the marvelous and the monstrous, the potential for human action is so mercurial here as to be of no consequence. Here, the psychic life of language holds open the poles of slavery's behavioral enterprise. The institution of slavery is truly what Coleridge sought in the demonic imagination: a beautiful but horrific sublime, a state wherein all possibility, imagined or otherwise, is managed and contained. Jefferson is Sula watching her mother burn, not out of spite but *interest*. Moreover, this passage is flooded with what I would call negative language about the category of the human. In Jefferson's piece, human exchange gives way to "commerce" and *any and all* human connection is arrested by a series of relations that makes the figures in Jefferson's hypothetical one with the machinery of slavery itself. The possibility of attaining or engaging in the kind of status bestowed upon the category "human" is withheld from everyone in Jefferson's short narrative and what we are left with are the "odious peculiarities" that also manage to thrive without a proper name.

Jefferson's poignant dismantling of the human through the perpetuation of a pervasive and therefore dominant narrative makes American slavery legible *only* as a fiction—and yet one worth preserving by any means necessary. The sexual practice of the nation's third president and the story at the root of *Gone With the Wind* are both haunted by touch: the image of Jefferson sleeping with (touching) Sally Hemings, or the idea of Scarlett O'Hara's (half) black sister putting her pen to paper (touching) the legacy of Scarlett and Rhett.[15] The prohibition against the touch extends even to the grave, as Jefferson's relatives and those of Sally Hemings continue to quarrel about the burial ground at Monticello. The idea of separate but equal ground annoyed descendants of Hemings, one of whom remarked, "Nothing's changed in two hundred years, has it?" On the other hand, John Work sent a letter to over seven hundred family members, "complaining that the lines between the two cemeteries 'would blur' over time and lead to 'a graveyard of Jefferson's descendants, *both real and imagined.*'"[16] Whiteness forms the stuff of the "real" and blackness is always already imagined territory. Jefferson's "white" relatives want to spare his legacy, his image from the "odious peculiarities" associated with slavery; his "black" relatives want to put an end to our understanding of such relations as "odious" or "peculiar" at all. When we think of slavery in America, we'd rather have the violent touch of enslaved bodies or the love that dare not speak its name—both "accounts" serve as romanticized fictions of past events. We are constantly hovering between these two inventions and are reminded that any attempt at the "truth" about slavery is simply unavailable to us. John Work's racism polices the border between black and white, male and female. At this contested border stands the body of a black woman; the fight over generation(s) and our claim upon it and them always enlists a gendered and raced standard.

If touch can be interpreted as the action that bars one from entry *and* also connects one to the sensual life of another, then we might go so far as to say that *racism has its own erotic life*. It is the particular legacy (if not genius) of the Confederacy that it was able to convince an entire nation to look toward the future for events that had already taken place in the past; to believe that emancipation would result in rampant miscegenation. Think about the kind of shame and then rage you might provoke when you ask someone to articulate the problem of racism (I am thinking of Du Bois here)—not from someone else's history but from their own. Even though property is everything in America, you will find difficulty in getting your neighbor to "own" this small piece of our collective pie.

Let me offer the following series of relationships. Our understanding of slavery as Americans vacillates among the good, the bad, and the ugly. Some see its touch as violent; others, like the purveyors of the legacy of Mitchell's novel, view "it" as doing more good than harm. Any attempt to revisit this myth called the past is likely to be viewed as just plain ugly. In Faulkner's imaginary the abrogation of the touch is precisely the problem: we are flailing at institutional structures like family, like race, without the proper implement; for Faulkner it is the touch that both sears the flesh and provides the opportunity for its suture.

"SO IT'S THE MISCEGENATION, NOT THE INCEST, WHICH YOU CANT BEAR"

The quotation that guides the argument in this section comes from the next to last chapter of *Absalom, Absalom!* The novel's signal and single investigative rationale goes without question and without answer, as Quentin's recounting of Sutpen's family saga continues at a furious pace while Shreve interjects his own interpretation of the events. In this moment, Quentin imagines Bon saying to Henry: "So it's the miscegenation, not the incest, which you cant bear" (293). Henry does not answer, because the sentence has no question mark. Moreover, because the question (or lack thereof) comes from all of the sons of the novel,[17] it stands without a proper host, without the "hospitality" or invitation that would let it loose on the chosen family; without the embodiment necessary to bring the word to fruition, or into flesh. That this question is never answered or asked in *Absalom, Absalom!* is perhaps the silence into which the last word on racism enters. So, too, racism's last word will never be the end of "it" surely, only a mark of its repudiation. Miscegenation, as the space of commingling and (un)like a vacuum, drags more than just race into its orbit. It also takes categories like brother/sister, human/animal, and produces an end product that is now the "us" that we used to call "them."

The absolute lack in which Faulkner's miscegenation/incest paradigm finds itself embedded is a measure of the tension between an emerging American model and an existing European model of the incest narrative; a model epitomized by the tragedy of Oedipus and trivialized in the Americas as a space without trauma or even the resolution that can result from remorse. If Oedipus blinds himself to the "truth" of his own sexual life, the American equivalent is not even on the horizon of appropriate responses of fear and shame. The response, articulated in Faulkner as silence—for it is a waste of time to tell someone what they always already know—is always "so what." It is revisited in Charles Bon's rambling love letter to his sister Judith. His words are filled with arrogant resignation:

> We have waited long enough. You will notice how I do not insult you either by saying I have waited long enough. And therefore, since I do not insult you by saying that only I have waited, I do not add, expect me. Because I cannot say when to expect me. Because what WAS is one thing, and now it is not because it is dead, it died in 1861, and therefore what IS . . . Because what IS is something else again because it was not even alive then. . . . I now believe that you and I are, strangely enough, included among those who are doomed to live. (108–9)

Bon regards his union with Judith as inevitable and therefore allies himself with a time that exists outside his own actions in the novel—his is an existential dilemma, fraught with erotic circumstance.

My call for a revised incest paradigm is by no means original, as Gilles Deleuze and Félix Guattari have signaled the end of the psychoanalytic mode of the Oedipus complex with their introduction of theories of the "anti-Oedipus" model.[18] But my desire to see a revised paradigm has as its rationale countless testimonials of recovered memories of incest trauma in the 1980s and 1990s—from published scholarly articles to talk show venues. It became patently clear that the "fact" of incest wasn't so much a problem for readers—and, in particular, audiences across the country—as their *reaction* to it. In an American Oedipal myth, the son wakes from his sister's bed and eyes you with defiance—a practiced nonchalance bred in the bosom of slavery's enterprise.[19] The "so what?" is loud, clear, and never cautious, never accompanied by the constant companion of wrongful transgression: contrition. What "survivors" and "victims" alike clamored for was an audience—someone to "listen," and in that listening acknowledge the problem and pain of incest. What they got was a stubborn refusal to see the danger in insouciance.[20]

In addition, and perhaps more radically, our conservative understanding of the incest paradigm also provides a neat separation between the human and the animal. Incest functions for the family much like race functions for the nation—both simultaneously keep and clean house. The problem is that incest and race do not and have not functioned as barriers between family members or nation-states; they are both tiny little fictions that preserve our sense of separateness and belonging.

Nothing disturbs the project of belonging more fully than the play at its outer boundary, where family and nation, in their more celebratory moments, stake a collective claim upon the difference between the human and the animal. In this register, a radical reading of Faulkner's work might prove fruitful. While Faulkner's work does indicate that his characters change very little over time—(there is no amazing grace in Faulkner's cosmos, only a pervasive relentlessness)—the status of the human as a principal site of inquiry is given less privilege than the *how* and the *what* (a cow, human chattel, an indecipherable ledger) of human interactions. Faulkner's human characters' attempt to demonstrate a range of human emotions, their obsession with a kaleidoscope of differences and their metaphorical equivalents, marks their journey in each narrative as wholly about something other than the human. The information that Faulkner's characters carry with them and the way they pass on the memory of slavery and removal (I am reminded of Jefferson's chapter on manners here) is to engage in certain practices, ritual and habitual, that circumscribe the human. At the same time, any *information* that we or the characters might have about the past is doomed to be lost in a present where such information is rendered useless. This problem is most recognizable in the extent to which a particularly American relationship to incest is emphasized in *Absalom, Absalom!*

At the end of the novel, we have to ask ourselves: What is the "it" that Quentin does not "hate"? The very end of the narrative suggests that there are humans interacting, dependent upon and independent of one another, but there is also a system—call it another narrative, call it the same one— that continues to trump what it means to be human altogether. Shreve is convinced that slavery is about human refuse: that the South is doomed is evidenced, not by practice but in and through the characters or bodies left in its wake. That Rosa and Quentin engage in a dance of listening and telling that is rendered obsolete by the structures of slavery that make the dance necessary in the first place is a point to which I now return. For Quentin, it is the *practice* (of slavery's economy, of incest's anti-Oedipal refrain) that continues, so as he attempts to tell the story and is constantly interrupted by Shreve, he is reminded of the practices of the slavocracy that give rise to his/our present circumstances. Although dated, Irving Howe's remarks upon the consciousness of white men in Faulkner's novels still have some resonance: "Beneath the white man's racial uneasiness there often beats an impatience with the devices by which men keep themselves apart. Ultimately the whole apparatus of separation must seem too wearisome in its constant call to alertness, too costly in its tax on the emotions, and simply tedious as a brake on spontaneous life."[21] Howe rightly identifies the gendered nature of black/white relationships in Faulkner's cosmos. Quentin's refusal to listen to Rosa's narrative is an indication of how slavery's remains are not about the human, as much as they are about systems, manners, and ultimately devastating practices. Perhaps this is why Rosa refers to her youth as "that warped and spartan solitude which I called my childhood, which had taught me (and little else) to listen before I could comprehend and to understand before I even heard" (116).

Unlike Rosa, Quentin is not bound to the reciprocation required by the act of storytelling. Faulkner writes:

> But Quentin was not listening, because there was also something which he too could not pass—that door, the running feet on the stairs beyond it almost a continuation of the fatal shot, the two women, the negress and the white girl in her underthings . . . pausing looking at the door, the yellowed creamy mass of old intricate satin and lace spread carefully on the bed . . . the two of them, brother and sister, curiously alike as if the difference in sex had merely sharpened the common blood to a terrific, an almost unbearable, similarity, speaking to one another in short brief staccato sentences like slaps. (142–43)

Quentin repudiates Rosa's word for the arrogance of his own. Had he listened to Rosa's story, he might have found a way out; a break in the constant rehearsal of the same practices that relegate the human in *Absalom, Absalom!* to the heap of remains created by slavery's enduring legacy.[22]

We have to remember that Quentin is not an agent of the past, he is only privy to its memory; he does not know what happened, so that the detail of the above scene merely announces a resurfacing of his own personal quagmire—his own desire to sleep with his sister. In fact, we could say that Quentin's only *desire* in *Absalom, Absalom!* is to extract meaning from the narrative that contributes to his own personal and incestuous quest. A quest marked by miscegenation as well.

Rosa's narrative—contained almost entirely in chapter 5 of the novel—is the absolute repudiation of the practices imbedded in slavery that allow for its continuance. For the characters in Faulkner's "human" tragedy, actions are preordained—subject not only to history (dismantled by modernism's blunt instrument) but also to other structures that exist in a time outside the novel's telling of "human" stories. In one of the novel's most important confrontations, Sutpen, during a "minute's exchange," *tells* rather than *asks* Rosa to be his wife. She recalls this "courtship" in two moments; the first: "He talking not about me or love or marriage, not even about himself and to no sane mortal listening nor out of any sanity, but to the very dark forces of fate which he had evoked and dared, out of that wild braggart dream where an intact Sutpen's Hundred which no more had actual being now . . . as though in the restoration of that ring to a living finger he had turned all time back twenty years and stopped it, froze it" (136). And the second: "I was (whatever it was he wanted of me—not my being, my presence: just my existence, whatever it was that Rosa Coldfield or any young female no blood kin to him represented in whatever it was he wanted—because I will do him this credit: he had never once thought about what he asked me to do until the moment he asked it)" (137). In both excerpts, "being" is interpreted as the house (Sutpen's Hundred) and the *absence* of Rosa, of the human subject altogether. Rosa's choice is a hard one; for as she violently rejects becoming Sutpen's common-law (and then, perhaps, legal) wife she experiences a simultaneous reification and absolute abjection: she gives up the right to become property for what is proper, only to become the very thing that she resists. In this scene, whiteness is categorically unable to transform one into a viable subject in the eyes of the larger community. The minute Rosa attempts to substantiate her whiteness, her difference (she is not Clytie, or Judith, or the now deceased Ellen), is the moment in which she loses her claim to that category. Rosa's earlier encounter with Clytie's touch, with the failure of the authority of whiteness, begins to inform her decision in this case. Regardless of her obsessive repudiation of it, the touch allows Rosa to *witness* her connection to Judith and to Clytie, so that when Sutpen returns and off-handedly does not ask but states that Rosa will marry him, she sees her fate as a white woman in relationship to the two women with whom she shared a house. The confluence of miscegenation, incest, and war catapults Rosa into a decision to step out of slavery's everyday life. As she recognizes this, she seems to repudiate being *like* Judith or Clytie—and this move initially appears as the preservation of white womanhood that we expect from Rosa. Sutpen's return, however, bears no acknowledgment of Rosa: Judith is "daughter" and Clytie retains the recognition of her name ("Ah, Clytie"), but for Rosa there is nothing but complete objectification and Sutpen's remedy to this predicament is to offer Rosa a marriage of sorts.

Sutpen's "touch" (or its absence) brings the erotic life of the novel to the forefront. For his command of marriage here indicates a continuance of past practices rather than a creation of a future contract or coupling. Rosa recalls the scene: "[He] came and stopped and put his hand on my head and (I do not know what he looked at while he spoke, save that by the sound of his voice it was not at us nor at anything in that room) said, 'You may think I made your sister Ellen no very good husband. You probably do think so. But even if you will not discount the fact that I am older now, I believe I can promise that I shall do no worse at least for you' " (135–36). It is a "ceremony" where Sutpen is "both groom and minister" (136). He has all the power of subjectivity, and for Rosa to become a wife she will have to accept all loss of meaning in such a title for herself and, as her memory ensures us, for all three women at Sutpen's Hundred. Moreover, she will also be unable to engender another generation that can inherit the gift of whiteness. Rosa goes to her fate as a picker, spinster, ghost with resignation —she loses the very whiteness that she so ardently defends from the beginning of chapter 5. It is the very practice of white female subjectivity and Rosa's desire for it that keeps the economics (blood, in this case) of slavery intact; Rosa discovers that a step outside of this economy surely entails the death of the subject, as she understands it, but it is a risk she is willing to take. And in doing so, Rosa becomes the perfect counterpart to Sutpen (a man obsessed with the practice of [racist] outrage): a woman who absolutely repudiates the substantiation of white subjectivity that racist practice requires. The residual effect of Rosa's renunciation is that she cannot reconcile herself with her own actions. Sutpen's touch—his own desire to continue racist practice—locks them both in the dance of racism's aftermath, as Rosa's rage toward Sutpen colors all relationships with him. With or without marriage or commingling, the erotic life of Sutpen's design and its repudiation determine the tenor of the novel. When Rosa and Sutpen enter the scene of proposal and potential coupling, Rosa is taken to the outer boundary of race and incest: she moves into the space of the human and animal; she sees the chattel she will become if she accepts Sutpen's vulgar offer, and also what she will be without it.

Between a rock and a hard place, Rosa accepts the inevitability of porousness—she understands the separation of white and black and, by extension, human and animal as not only impossible but dangerous. In the seams of this narrative is that racial shibboleth, to which we have become so accustomed that resisting it is futile. When we pay attention to the erotic life of racism, we move onto another playing field altogether where we must abandon the positions that hold white and black being in such static relation.

On the staircase or in the parking lot, we mark the time/space continuum of our belonging. Cars, people, children, come and go on that same pavement where this book began, and I do not know whether the Safeway has been leveled for another strip mall or if it stands still, beckoning us to some version of the quotidian in which we all share. In our reiterations of slavery's several endeavors, it is time to write a new chapter of our relation(s) as truly interdisciplinary, where the dangerous work of the everyday has some transformative (phenomenological?) agency. This book is just one attempt to remember what quotidian moves we must make in order to contain our racial feeling, and how the *work* of racism is important to that practice. To bring us back to a beginning of sorts, "You can't be what you were / So you better start being / just what you are."[23]

Notes

INTRODUCTION

The subtitle of this introduction is taken from a translation of the title of Jacques Derrida's essay "Racism's Last Word." Parts of this chapter and the conclusion were published as "The Last Word on Racism: New Directions in Critical Race Theory," South Atlantic Quarterly 104, no. 3 (2005): 403–23.

1. The term "critical race theory" reflects its indebtedness to and significant departure from the Frankfurt school's Marxist cohort. For an analysis of the important legal theory behind the critical race theory movement, see Crenshaw et al., eds., *Critical Race Theory*. In the introduction to the volume, the editors write that "although Critical Race scholarship differs in object, argument, accent, and emphasis, it is nevertheless unified by two common interests. The first is to understand how a regime of white supremacy and its subordination of people of color have been created and maintained in America, and, in particular, to examine the relationship

between that social structure and professed ideals such as 'the rule of law' and 'equal protection.' The second is a desire not merely to understand the vexed bond between law and racial power but to *change* it" (xiii). By rejecting the idea that the aim of intellectual work should be objectivity, critical race theory maps the possibilities for intimate connection between author and subject, community and academic enterprise. See also Richard Delgado and Jean Stefancic who in *Critical Race Theory* make the claim that "racism is ordinary, not aberrational" (7).

2. The FBI exhumed the body of Emmett Till from its Alsip, Illinois, burial spot in 2005 after federal prosecutors reopened the investigation into his 1955 murder. Investigators found that an autopsy had never been performed on Till's body at the time of his death and that the cause of death had never been determined. A documentary film about the murder suggested that forensic evidence links others besides the defendants Roy Bryant and J. W. Milam to his death. Bryant and Milam were acquitted of Till's murder by an all-white jury, but later told *Look* magazine that they were responsible for it. See Monica Davey and Gretchen Ruethling, "After 50 Years, Emmett Till's Body is Exhumed," *New York Times*, June 2, 2005; Debra Pickett, "Till's Well-Preserved Body Exhumed: Autopsy Planned in Federal Probe of Boy's 1955 Murder," *Chicago Sun-Times*, June 2, 2005; Gretchen Ruethling, "F.B.I. Will Exhume the Body of Emmett Till for an Autopsy," *New York Times*, May 5, 2005, and "Kin Disagree on Exhumation of Emmett Till," *New York Times*, May 6, 2005; Kyle Martin, "FBI Defends Its Decision to Exhume Till's Body," *Greenwood Commonwealth*, May 16, 2005; and Shaila Dewan, "A Crescendoing Choir from the Graveyards of History," *New York Times*, August 21, 2005.

On the 1998 dragging death of James Byrd Jr. in Jasper, Texas, see Carol Marie Cropper, "Black Man Fatally Dragged in Possible Racial Killing," *New York Times*, June 10, 1998 and "Town Expresses Sadness and Horror over Slaying," *New York Times*, June 11, 1998; Rick Lyman, "Man Guilty of Murder in Texas Dragging Death," *New York Times*, February 24, 1999, and "Texas Jury Picks Death Sentence in Fatal Dragging of Black Man," *New York Times*, February 26, 1999; "Trial Begins for Second Suspect in Dragging Death," *New York Times*, September 14, 1999; "Second Man on Death Row in Dragging of Black Man," *New York Times*, September 24, 1999; and "Third Defendant Is Convicted in Dragging Death in Texas," *New York Times*, November 19, 1999.

3. Miles and Brown, *Racism*, 88. See also Grosz, *The Nick of Time*, for a discussion of our misconception of Darwin's famed notion of "survival of the fittest" and its relationship to time, gender, and race.

4. Toni Morrison, *Beloved*, 190.

5. In thinking through law and custom, Charles Mills observes that "the Racial Contract establishes a racial polity, a racial state, and a racial juridical system, where the status of whites and nonwhites is clearly demarcated, whether by law or custom.

And the purpose of this state, by contrast with the neutral state of classic contractarianism, is, inter alia, specifically to maintain and reproduce this racial order, securing the privileges and advantages of the full white citizens and maintaining the subordination of nonwhites" (*The Racial Contract*, 14). I can think of no better interlocutor for Mills than the work of David Theo Goldberg in studies such as *Racist Culture*, *The Racial State*, and *Anatomy of Racism*. *Racist Culture* is a graduate-school primer on racism, the Enlightenment, and how racist exclusions perpetuate structural inequalities. *The Racial State* is an extension of the first book and focuses on the state as the arbiter of racial expression. *Anatomy of Racism* is an edited volume with contributions from Kwame Anthony Appiah, Lucius Outlaw, Frantz Fanon, Nancy Leys Stepan, Roland Barthes, Julia Kristeva, and Sander L. Gilman, among others. Goldberg's effort in this text seems to be to outline the various contours of "race talk" (xi).

6. Piper, "Passing for White, Passing for Black," 250.

7. Gillian Harkins in *Everybody's Family Romance* proposes that we pay attention to the "latent radicalism of 1990s narratives" (9). In her introduction she writes: "The book reads incest as a trope bridging changing formations of U.S. nationalism, one that exploits the modern coupling of family and nation to recode violence and hegemony in formations of emergent social life. Thus I argue that incest both reveals hidden forms of gendered violence and lends itself to new hegemonic forms of domestic consumption. But this book also reads incest as a trope able to interrupt this revelatory hegemony, stealing away from the enclosures of either residual forms of nationalism or emergent forms of social organization" (4). Harkins takes seriously Michael Hardt and Antonio Negri's charge in *Empire* that in order to unseat the particularly dangerous hold that neoliberalism has had on contemporary political culture, new narratives and aesthetic interventions must be brought to life. See in particular Harkins's assessment of how a "refunctioned incest trope might be used to remake the generational borders of kinship" in chapter 5, "Consensual Relations: The Scattered Generations of Kinship" (188). Her review of the Rind study should be of particular interest to scholars working in fields across race, sex, gender, and sexuality. I return to a discussion of antineoliberal thought in chapter 3.

8. Kwame Anthony Appiah calls this particular predicament "cognitive incapacity" ("Racisms," 6). For Appiah, this means that even when one is confronted with overwhelming evidence that one's beliefs are invalid, one will still hold onto archaic forms of knowledge, especially if such knowledge requires a reflection upon one's own self-image or, more drastically, a shift in the redistribution of wealth or privilege.

9. In their guest column for *PMLA*, "What Does Queer Theory Teach Us about X?," Lauren Berlant and Michael Warner conclude that "queer commentary has

tried to drive into visibility both the cultural production of sexuality and the social context of feeling" (347).

10. Robert Reid-Pharr's work in *Conjugal Union* and *Once You Go Black* makes him one of this generation's most important critics of the black intellectual tradition. It is a shame that for Reid-Pharr the black intellectual is always already figured as male, thereby making his provocative and insightful musings rigorously gendered and, as such, less useful to other companion projects. Nevertheless, the sentiments expressed in *Once You Go Black* parallel many of my observations here about how blackness is taken to be understood from within and without. As Reid-Pharr notes, "neither Black American identity nor racialized oppression exempted one from participation in the maintenance—and *re*articulation—of the main structures of society, including those structures that work to oppress oneself and ones community" (41). Reid-Pharr's work urges us to reevaluate our insistence of the black subject's embeddedness—in community and in our narratives about it. As Reid-Pharr pronounced in *Conjugal Union*, "I reject the notion that the black body is some species of the always already . . . During the antebellum period intellectuals began the arduous, awkward process of establishing the peculiarity of the black body, the distinctiveness that could never be exorcised. I utilize the already impossibly overdetermined notion of black embodiment, then, to refer, not to some demonstrable physical fact, but to a specifically American ideological effect in which race is always produced on a two-dimensional black/white axis" (6). My work returns to the production of that binary and the static situationality of black being to understand what is lost and what is gained by holding "it" captive in such restrictive critical sights.

11. Spillers, *Black, White, and in Color*, 208.

12. Michael Jackson, "Wanna Be Starting Something," *Thriller* (1982).

13. Constitutive of this shift away from race to racism is also an overwhelming need to break "with the black-white racism problematic" and instead focus on what Antonia Darder and Rodolfo Torres describe as "how best to conceptualize multiple racisms and racialized formations within the context of demographic shifts, changing capitalist class relations, and global socioeconomic dislocations" (*After Race*, 3).

14. Gilroy, *Against Race*, 15.

15. I use the word "junction" here purposefully, as I want to call attention to the "thingness" of both categories. Belief in "black" and "white" as essence is a belief in the impossibility of their commingling. I want to call attention to the fact that their joined state is always already about their objectification as things, not persons. In Gayatri Chakravorty Spivak's assessment of Jack Forbes's *Black Africans and Native Americans* she finds promise in his urgent request for us to see that the racially inflected nomenclature of "conquest" and settlement dismantles the efficacy of the

black-white binary. Such promise relates to our ability to confront "today's black-white (or different-same) liberal multiculturalism" ("Race before Racism," 48). But while the argument here is that this binary might obscure other persons, this binary nevertheless continues to have psychic salience because we seem to understand black-white interactions as *doing* the same thing over and over in the kinds of stories we tell and interpretations we give to their relation.

16. See the coverage in the *New York Times* of the Congressional Black Caucus and the presidential candidacy of Barack Obama, notably Matt Bai, "Is Obama the End of Black Politics?," *New York Times*, August 6, 2008. In this article Bai discusses the generational divide among black leaders over Obama's candidacy, highlighted in particular by an exchange between Rev. Jesse Jackson and his son, Jesse Jackson Jr. The latter, who was national co-chairman of Obama's campaign, said he was "deeply outraged and disappointed" by his father's comment in July 2008 that he wouldn't mind castrating Obama. The comment was sparked, according to news coverage at the time, by Jackson's anger over Obama's admonishment of black fathers during a Father's Day speech, and his "talking down to black people." For more on this issue, see Perry Bacon, "Jackson Incident Revives Some Blacks' Concerns about Obama," *Washington Post*, July 11, 2008. See also Sheryl Gay Stolberg, "For Obama, Nuance on Race Invites Questions," *New York Times*, February 8, 2010, which discusses responses from black scholars, politicians, policymakers, and members of the media to Obama's handling of the "race issue" and his dedication to the black community. See also Jonathan Weisman, "Rev. Jackson Apologizes to Obama," *Washington Post*, July 10, 2008; and John Kass, "Obama Backers on the Left Are Doing the Wincing Now," *Chicago Tribune*, July 13, 2008.

17. Nietzsche might not seem to be the best philosophic interlocutor to my ideas here, but Robert Gooding-Williams in "Supposing Nietzsche to Be Black—What Then?" in his book *Look, a Negro!*, has noted that his work can be useful for antiracist endeavors. As Gooding-Williams writes: "Because Nietzsche declines to flatter European culture, but represents it as the contingent, overdetermined product of slave morality, cruelty, decadence, and nihilism, he remains a useful model for any thinker—indeed, for any African American thinker—who would puncture European or now Euro-American pieties in order to date and imagine alternatives to the Eurocultrual legacies of white supremacy. Nietzsche's colonialist fantasies can be a guide in this endeavor, for they repeatedly implicate his demystifying criticisms of European culture" (132). Even Jacqueline Scott proceeds with some caution: "Nietzsche might seem to be a counter intuitive source for contemporary race theorists, but he undertook the task of healing his culture by revaluing the prevailing concept of race" ("The Price of the Ticket," 151). And as James Winchester observes: "Nietzsche was clearly very interested in concept of race. The word appears more than two hundred times in the Colli-Montinari edition of Nietzsche's

work. It also appears frequently in his letters . . . [he] is not the racist that some claim that he is, but he does at times adopt some of the thinking on race that was prevalent in his own time but is now widely questioned" ("Nietzsche's Racial Profiling," 255). See also Preston, "Nietzsche on Blacks."

18. Saidiya Hartman in *Scenes of Subjection* has offered us a way to think through pleasure as an impossibility, thus continuing what I will argue in chapter 2 is a strong black feminist commitment to disarticulate pleasure from scenes of subjection. Fred Moten in his critique of the sounding voice in *In the Break* has thought to reimagine Hartman's work. In his analysis of Aunt Hester's scream and engagement of Hartman's reading of it, Moten notes that "Douglass's *is* a primal scene for complex reasons that have to do with the connectedness of desire, identification, and castration that Hartman displaces onto the field of the mundane and the quotidian, where pain is alloyed with pleasure. However, this displacement somehow both acknowledges and avoids the vexed question of the possibility of pain and pleasure mixing in the scene and in its originary and subsequent recountings" (4; emphasis in original). I wholeheartedly agree with Moten's view of pain and pleasure as mixed feelings, and I understand his revision of Hartman's work to open up a space toward the nature of the quotidian within scenes of subjection as a fruitful critical mode.

19. Nyong'o, "Punk'd Theory," 30.

20. Beauvoir, *The Second Sex*, 56.

21. I use the word "modes" here purposefully as it signals behavior that is automatic or habitual. My use of the term "erotic" does not anchor itself in the psychoanalytic but rather fluctuates between dictionary definitions of the words "desire" and "erotic." This project is located between the object relations inherent in "desire"—a wish for something—and the way in which sexuality is inextricable from the erotic itself.

22. Halle, *Queer Social Philosophy*, 117.

23. Hames-García, "Can Queer Theory Be Critical Theory?," 216.

24. This observation is, of course, indebted to Fanon's undertakings in *Black Skin, White Masks*, where he remarks, "I occupied space" (quoted in Gibson, "Losing Sight of the Real," 133) in a rather dramatic passage about the signification of blackness in the context of colonization. This indebtedness to Fanon in understandings of the time/space continuum is not explored in Elizabeth Grosz's first critical endeavor, *Space, Time and Perversion*. I point this out here because in much of the work by philosophers interested in race any talk of being, time, and psychoanalysis seems to warrant an examination of or at least a cursory nod to Fanon and his contribution to understandings of subjectivity. See also Henry, "African and Afro-Caribbean Existential Philosophies"; and Barrett, *Blackness and Value*.

25. Quoted in McBride, "Introduction," 8.

26. See Holland, "The Beached Whale."

27. Faulkner, *Absalom, Absalom!*, 115.

28. I want to thank the undergraduates in my Queer Theory class at the University of Illinois, Chicago, for their thoughtful engagement with contemporary theory and for teaching me how to become a better teacher and reader of complex work. I want also to thank the graduate students in my Critical Race Theory class at Northwestern University (fall 2007), whose love for the "racial" project helped me to find a way to respectfully dismantle our positively charged racial feeling.

29. In 2003, discussions at two conferences erupted into furious debate. "The Ends of Sexuality: Pleasure and Danger in the New Millennium" (April) at Northwestern and "Gay Shame" (March) at Michigan proved that when we get around to the business of hating each other we tend to do it very well indeed. In another register, Hiram Perez's scathing critique of the "Gay Shame" conference has great resonance with this project. In seeking to unearth the definition of "brown" within the confines of a stereotypical rendering of a gay brown body, Perez locates "brown" as ambiguous but acknowledges its emergence out of "the prevailing black/white opposition of U.S. race discourse"—a blackness here that is marked for "white dominant culture" as a way to "sustain the impossibility of a private black sexuality" ("You Can Have My Brown Body and Eat It, Too!," 186). The black/white opposition here is conceived of as a problem for theorizing away from identity's embeddedness. Yet, the brown body heralds the recognition of the black body's lack of privacy. While the goal here is not to unpack the various permutations of black, brown, and white, it is clear from Perez's piece that some accounting for if not rearticulation of the boundary between black and white is necessary in order to begin to tell a different story of their relationship.

30. Spillers, "Mama's Baby, Papa's Maybe," 231; emphasis mine.

1. RACE

1. Lindon Barrett's *Blackness and Value*, an excellent contribution to the analysis of race, gender, and sexuality in African American literature, is often overlooked by many literary critics. Michelle Maria Wright in *Becoming Black* links the work of Hegel, Gobineau, and Jefferson to furthering interpretations of the "Negro" and its place in Western chronologies of being.

2. Faulkner, *Absalom, Absalom!*, 143.

3. I am not the first critic to find horse and rider analogies interesting. See Freud, *The Ego and the Id*, notably his reference to the relationship between the two. He writes: "Thus in [the ego's] relation to the id it is like a man on horseback, who has to hold in check the superior strength of the horse; with this difference, that the rider tries to do so with his own strength while the ego uses borrowed forces. The analogy may be carried a little further. Often a rider, if he is not to be parted from

his horse, is obliged to guide it where it wants to go; so in the same way the ego is in the habit of transforming the id's will into action as if it were its own" (15). The ego essentially mediates the id and super-ego. Thus, two primary components of ego are a system of perception and a set of unconscious (specifically, preconscious) ideas. Its relationship to the unconscious id, therefore, is a close one. The ego must control the id, like the rider, but at times the rider is obliged to guide the horse where it wants to go. Likewise, the ego must, at times, negotiate the desires of the id. Finally, the ego is "that part of the id which has been modified by the direct influence of the external world" (15). It is this idea of perception that leads Freud to call the ego a "body ego" (17)—a mental projection of the surface of one's physical body. These ideas of the body, perception, and materiality are thoroughly explored in Jay Prosser's *Second Skins*. I am indebted to Carole-Anne Tyler for her contributions to my understanding here via an e-mail exchange on July 29, 2010.

4. Bonilla-Silva, *Racism without Racists*, 124.

5. One can see the beginnings of a discourse below skin level as early as 1985 in Dorothy Nelkin and Susan Lindee's "The Media-ted Gene." The most recent foray into the territory of genomics and epidemiology is Priscilla Wald's *Contagious*.

6. Darder and Torres, *After Race*, 100.

7. Richeson and Shelton, "Negotiating Interracial Interactions," 316, 319.

8. Sikka, "Heidegger and Race," 91.

9. Hall, "What Is This 'Black' in Black Popular Culture?," 472.

10. Among the key players in critical race theory are Kimberlé Crenshaw, Anthony Appiah, Philomena Essed, Howard Winant, Toni Morrison, Michael Omi, Cathy Cohen, Robert Miles, Malcolm Brown, Paul Gilroy, Robyn Wiegman, David Theo Goldberg, Wahneema Lubiano, Charles Mills, Eduardo Bonilla-Silva, Satya Mohanty, David Roediger, and Paula Moya. Although these individuals are by no means all the players on the field, for me they represent the interdisciplinary nature of scholarly work on race as well as many of its most important epistemological tracks. All of these scholars have contributed to one or more of the following articulations: the social construction of race, the problem of racism, and in particular, the place of "blackness" within modernity's emerging racialized aesthetic. Although not all of these scholars will be examined in depth in this chapter, each is responsible for a substantial intervention (whether we like it or not) in the discourse about race. This list purposefully leaves out writers such as Dinesh D'Souza, Shelby Steele, James McWhorter, and Thomas Sowell, among others. Although their work on race has been influential as it corroborates common feelings about race in the context of the United States, the *scholarly* aspects of their work leave much to be desired. Most of these writers rely upon specious claims about racial identities, or disregard entirely the available research, empirical and qualitative, on the subject of race.

Much of Appiah's influence upon the discourse of race and racism stems from his bold reading of W. E. B. Du Bois's "The Conservation of the Races." In this reading he interprets the thrust of Du Bois's signature text and its plan for African American participation in the polity of the United States as in *collusion* with scientific racism's dependence upon the biological as social determinant. See also Bernasconi, introduction to *Race and Racism in Continental Philosophy*; Sundstrom, "Douglass and Du Bois' Der Schwarze Volksgeis"; and Essed, *Understanding Everyday Racism*. Much like the postpositive realist theorists Paula Moya (*Learning from Experience*) and Linda Alcoff ("The Problem of Speaking for Others"), Essed wants to make experience, in particular "black" experience, central to her study of racism in the European context. Her interdisciplinary work focuses primarily upon the Netherlands, and she defines racism "in terms of cognitions, actions, and procedures that contribute to the development and perpetuation of a system in which Whites dominate Blacks" (39). See Omi and Winant, *Racial Formation in the United States*; Morrison, *Playing in the Dark*; Lubiano, *The House That Race Built*; and Roediger "White Workers, New Democrats, and Affirmative Action." See also Wing, *Global Critical Race Feminism*, which is especially focused on legal studies.

11. See Crenshaw, "Mapping the Margins"; and Cohen, "Punks, Bulldaggers, and Welfare Queens."

12. Crenshaw, "Mapping the Margins," 1245.

13. Intersectionality has become something that black feminists "do" by default. For a time in the 1980s it didn't matter if you were working on "intersectionality" directly or not; if you appeared to be a black feminist, you were assumed to be working on it. By the same token, a nod to intersectionality in any feminist conference paper was assumed to represent a whole host of theorists in exchange for actual engagement. In chapter 3, I find Jasbir Puar's nod to "intersectionality" interesting precisely for these reasons—it is the psychic life of the term that appeals to me here.

A comprehensive history of intersectionality does not exist, but it has its roots in sociological methodologies and was popularized by Patricia Hill Collins. A good example of the default position on intersectionality can be found in Sara Ahmed, *Queer Phenomenology*: "We can recall here the importance of 'intersectionality' to black feminist theory. Given that relationships of power 'intersect,' how we inhabit a given category depends on how we inhabit others" (136).

14. One of the most cogent contextualizations of Crenshaw's method can be found in McCall's "The Complexity of Intersectionality." In *After Race*, Darder and Torres attempt to interrogate intersectionality, but make no effort to cite Crenshaw let alone argue with her (see, in particular, chapter 5, "What's So Critical about Critical Race Theory?"). In addition, Paul Gilroy calls for "far more patient and careful attention to issues of gender and sexuality than critics have been inclined to

do so far" (*Against Race*, 182), but in his analysis of hip hop and reference to Henry Louis Gates's now infamous defense of 2 Live Crew, he makes no mention of Crenshaw's invaluable critique of this very public critical misstep on the part of Gates. A more recent investigation of intersectionality's long reach is Jennifer Nash's "Re-Thinking Intersectionality." In a section titled "The Theoretical Importance of Black Women," Nash observes that "intersectionality's reliance on black women as the basis for its claims to complex subjectivity renders black women prototypical intersectional subjects whose experiences of marginality are imaged to provide a *theoretical value-added*" (8).

15. Crenshaw, "Mapping the Margins," 1296.

16. Denise Ferreira da Silva is similarly vexed by Foucault's inability to think through the relationship of race and sexuality. As she writes: "What prevents Foucault from fully incorporating the nineteenth-century concept of the racial in his critique of modern thought, I think, is not an empirical limitation—though such limitations are significant, as indicated in Stoler's (1995) examination of how the discourse of race participates in the formation of bourgeois European sexuality— but his partial engagement with modern representation" (*Toward a Global Idea of Race*, 25). Lynne Huffer intervenes in critical discussions of Foucault's use of "history" with a reimagining of the place of his *History of Madness* in our critical repertoire. In sum, Huffer wants scholars of feminism and queer theory in particular to return to this text and view it as foundational, as Foucault's views of history are mapped out in this crucial but all but forgotten text. As she writes: "Foucault's most important contribution to the question of how to think about the past [is that] he understood the philosophical work of history making as fraught negotiation between the present and the future whose purpose is to bring that which is 'irreparably less than history' into view. Doing so, he made a commitment to a different time" (*Mad for Foucault*, 19). In chapter 3, Huffer goes on to challenge mistranslations of Foucault's more playful language in *Sexuality One*, queer theory's ur-text.

17. See Stone, "Sisterhood Is Powerful." See also Robin Morgan, *Sisterhood Is Powerful*.

18. Cohen, "Punks, Bulldaggers, and Welfare Queens," 25.

19. This move to ground queer studies—to have it acknowledge its indebtedness to women of color in particular—is starting to make shifts, not in queer theory but in feminist historicizations of the second wave. Chief among these reenvisionings of the second wave is Kimberly Springer's *Living for the Revolution*. In addition, see Rosalyn Baxandall's "Re-visioning the Women's Liberation Movement's Narrative" and Brian Norman's " 'We' in Redux." Both Baxandall and Norman reevaluate the content of early black feminist organizations and statements with the aim to reimagine their importance in the formation rather than the contribution to second

wave discourse. I thank Robyn Wiegman for introducing me to their writings, which have been invaluable to my work on second wave feminism both inside and outside the classroom.

20. This movement in queer studies was first embarked upon by José Muñoz with the publication of *Disidentifications*, which takes Gramsci's notion of the "organic intellectual" seriously with splendid and provocative results. The second wave of queer of color critique came about with *Aberrations in Black*, Rod Ferguson's move to rethink the place of "capital" in queer critique while simultaneously focusing upon the golden age of women of color feminism. A special edition of *Social Text* from 2005, "What's Queer about Queer Studies Now," centers queer of color critique by providing an opportunity for scholars to bolster the emerging discourse with their own readings. While much has been said about queer of color critique, its relationship to black queer studies in particular remains to be articulated. The fundamental question is if black queer studies used black feminist paradigms in its analysis of the efficacy of queer critical strategies, how is queer of color critique different from black queer studies? One obvious difference is the explicit engagement with historical materialism that is at the heart of the work in queer of color critique.

21. Hortense Spillers, however, is the notable exception. Although she does call for a genderless space in "Mama's Baby, Papa's Maybe," it is not with the same results for a discourse on race. I will be examining Spillers's contributions more closely in chapter 3.

22. Walter Benn Michaels would consider himself a member of this latter camp, and he would add that arguments of race over class contribute to the very thing that antiracist discourse is supposed to prevent: the cementing of cultural norms *as* ontological truths. See the now infamous exchange in *Critical Inquiry* between Michaels and Avery Gordon and Christopher Newfield: Michaels, "Race into Culture: A Critical Genealogy of Cultural Identity"; Gordon and Newfield, "White Philosophy"; and Michaels, "The No Drop Rule." Darder and Torres in *After Race* both observe that "race-centered scholars have unwittingly perpetuated the vacuous and dangerous notion that politics and economics are two separate spheres of society which function independently—a view that firmly anchors and sustains prevailing class relations of power in society" (106–7). Michaels is in no way the originator of the "class over race" paradigm—in the late 1970s William Julius Wilson in *The Declining Significance of Race* put forth the proposition that class might matter more than race. One could even say that the struggle between race and culture began with the depoliticization of race in Britain, a moment that Robert Miles and Malcolm Brown as well as Satya Mohanty recognize as signal in the development of contemporary ideologies of race and culture. See Miles and Brown, *Racism*; and Mohanty, *Literary Theory and the Claims of History*, 17.

23. Miles and Brown in *Racism* consistently refer to Gilroy's *Between Camps*. Many of the concepts in this citation are echoed in Gilroy's *Against Race*.

24. I will have more to say about materiality and queer theory in chapter 2, when I redact Jay Prosser's response in *Second Skins* to Butler's use of transsexual identity as a key signifier of queer being.

25. See Duggan, *The Twilight of Equality*, and Muñoz, *Cruising Utopia*, for brilliant redactions of neoliberalism's effects. See also Jasbir Puar's seeringly accurate mapping of neoliberalism's discourse in *Terrorist Assemblages*. Puar writes very persuasively, that "a pernicious binary . . . has emerged in the post–civil rights era in legislative, activist, and scholarly realms: the homosexual other is white, the racial other is straight" (32).

26. Miles and Brown later view this black/white dichotomy as the cause of a commonly held idea that "racism is conceived as something that 'white' people think about and do to 'black' people" (*Racism*, 68).

27. I say this while fully recognizing that Miles and Brown intend *Racism* to be a transatlantic perspective: Miles teaches at the University of North Carolina, Chapel Hill, and Brown teaches at the University of Exeter.

28. See Bryce Traister's discussion of the transnational and American studies in "The Object of Study."

29. See David Theo Goldberg and Philomena Essed's introduction to *Race Critical Theories*. In their call to broaden the approach of critical legal race theory in the United States, Goldberg and Essed remark that it is "marked by an American parochialism, with being caught up with more or less restricted considerations of legal structures, conditions and rationalities in the U.S. context. Scant attention is paid either to the applicability and implications of its key concepts outside of that context, or perhaps more importantly (because more constitutively) to thinking its central concepts through their globalizing significance and circulation" (4–5). My issue here is not with their call to thinking beyond the borders of the United States but rather that such scholarship is always already global when it thinks about the United States as perforated by many nations—native American communities— which have a rich history of critical race work among them (see Miles and Holland, *Crossing Waters, Crossing Worlds* for a reconceptualization of diaspora). Moreover, this call to look outward often puts the onus on the intellectual traditions of people of color in the United States to take on the psychic responsibility of United States exceptionalism.

30. Elsewhere, Miles has noted that there is no such thing as race and therefore no "race relations," thereby citing a familiar argument in social science circles that those who perpetuate the efficacy of the term "race" are responsible for extending its shelf life by continuing to employ it as a real category of analysis (*Racism after "Race Relations,"* 90).

31. Bonilla-Silva in his first chapter of *Racism without Racists* (12–13) describes his data sources as the Survey of Social Attitudes of College Students (1997) and the Detroit Area Study (1998).

32. Bonilla-Silva, *Racism without Racists*, 53.

33. As Bonilla-Silva writes: "Whites interpreted the past as slavery, even when in some questions we left it open (e.g., questions regarding the 'history of oppression') or we specified we were referring to 'slavery and Jim Crow' " (ibid., 79).

34. Ibid., xv.

35. Quoted in ibid., 172. It is important to note that Bonilla-Silva's take on Omi and Winant is a bit more trenchant than most. For example, Lucius Outlaw credits (as do others) Omi and Winant with bringing our attention to the "racial state" and race as a "formation" within it. Outlaw argues that this approach preserves "race" as a viable category of analysis because of Omi and Winant's attention to its social and historical construction within the give and take of social struggle. See Outlaw, "Toward a Critical Theory of 'Race,' " 77.

36. Bonilla-Silva, *Racism without Racists*, 173.

37. Ibid., 179. Charles Mills also takes note of the importance of "browns" in racial hierarchies in Latin America. He cautions us to understand that this tripartite system does not alter the kind of power that whiteness wields in a society or change the social status of those at the bottom. See his *Blackness Visible*, especially chapter 5, "Revisionist Ontologies: Theorizing White Supremacy."

38. Edelman, *No Future*, 3.

39. Bonilla-Silva, *Racism without Racists*, 9.

40. Mills, *The Racial Contract*, 1; emphasis mine.

41. Ibid., 7. For a detailed reading of their role in the development of contract theory, see 64–72.

42. I once was asked by a colleague in a philosophy department I was visiting if I thought that *The Racial Contract* was weak philosophically. I have always thought of that question as resting upon another set of assumptions—namely, that philosophical inquiry (always an inquiry about *it*self) is inherently sound, or put another way, that the intellectual genealogy that philosophy employs to traverse its own trajectory is *the way* to speak about all things philosophical.

43. Mills, *The Racial Contract*, 11.

44. Ibid., 14.

45. See Wiegman, *American Anatomies*, 27.

46. It is beyond the scope of this project to outline the differences between analytical and continental philosophy approaches to race, but it is commonly held that the analytical approach is less fruitful than the continental approach. For a review of these methods, see Robert Bernasconi's introduction to *Race and Racism in Continental Philosophy*. Bernasconi's argument *for* continental philosophy as a

better instrument for the task of dismantling race has to do with his commitment to a certain rigor that his approach can sustain, as it relies upon actual readings of the key philosophical texts rather than redactions of arguments within them that can be proven, disproven, or dismissed. As he explains: "The recent explosion of interest in race theory among philosophers in English-speaking countries has so far been largely dominated by philosophers whose training and frame of reference is that of analytic philosophy. That marks a certain limitation not only in the resources available to them, but also in the questions discussed. The focus falls on the reality of the concept of race, its relation to biology, and such questions as whether racism implies a belief in race. Other questions, such as the relation of race to culture, to history, and to one's sense of self, which have long been discussed by Black philosophers throughout the world, have not been at the forefront of recent research in race theory" (1).

47. Gossett, *Race*, 29. Gossett goes on to reiterate the widely held belief that justifications for slavery of "Negroes and Indians" rested upon *religious* rather than biological differences. It is my contention that this kind of caution in discourse about race anticipates and responds to the specious claim of separatist black nationalist thought which can present a totalizing teleology of race and racism. I want to thank Dwight McBride for bringing Gossett's work to my attention.

48. Marlon Ross in "Beyond the Closet as a Raceless Paradigm" takes issue with Wiegman's theory of knowledge formation and race as an organizing principle: "If we take seriously both Foucault's argument that the identity of modern homosexuality tends to be totalized as a singular species, and Wiegman's argument that race becomes the primary organizing principle of modernity at least a century earlier, then we arrive at a theoretical-historical impasse. If by the eighteenth century, race is already marked on "the body" as a totalizing sign of invisible anatomical species difference, then what happens in the nineteenth century, when, as Foucault argues, homosexuality is marked on 'the body' as a totalizing sign of invisible anatomical species difference? Are Wiegman and Foucault talking about two totally different bodies?" (165). Ross's question is an important one. The problem of history outlined here still seems to haunt the margins of queer studies work.

49. Wiegman, *American Anatomies*, 27.

50. Mills, *The Racial Contract*, 61.

51. Ibid., 18. Mills elaborates upon his concept of epistemological ignorance with the following gesture: "Whites will then act in racist ways while thinking of themselves as acting morally. In other words, they will experience genuine cognitive difficulties in recognizing certain behavior patterns *as* racist, so that quite apart from questions of motivation and bad faith, they will be morally handicapped simply from the conceptual point of view in seeing and doing the right thing. As I emphasized at the start, the Racial Contract prescribes, as a condition for membership in the polity, an epistemology of ignorance" (*The Racial Contract*, 93). I

contend here that the same cognitive difficulty arises when anyone thinks race instead of racist practice. Thus, black subjects who eschew amalgamation with white subjects in order to safeguard black culture are equally susceptible to "racist" action, regardless of whether such actions have global or local impact.

52. Kwame Anthony Appiah sees "racism as the practice of reasonable human beings" ("Racisms," 4). Appiah also suggests that racialism—the belief that there are "heritable characteristics, possessed by members of our species, that allow us to divide them into a small set of races, in such a way that all members of these races share certain traits and tendencies with each other that they do not share with members of any other race"—was practiced and believed by some even before nineteenth-century racialist science (5). All of this is an indication that although we tend to understand race along a narrative of progression, the views to substantiate the science of race were in circulation long before its fruition.

53. Wiegman, *American Anatomies*, 35.

54. Wiegman as well as Mills relies upon what she calls this "binary cleavage of race" to mine the events that continue to reify such oppositionality (ibid., 40). Like Mills, Wiegman does want to site white supremacy: "Ours is a white supremacist system asymmetrical in its economic and political allotments, triumphant in its ability to mask deep disparity on the one hand, and yet thoroughly rigid in its maintenance of naïve individualism and rhetorical democracy on the other" (41–42). The differences between them are slight. Nevertheless, they both see white supremacy as having a significant hand in racial formation.

55. Ibid., 84–85.

56. Mills's book does, however, delimit female gender—he borrows his title from Carole Pateman's *The Sexual Contract*. In answer to critics on this issue, Pateman and Mills jointly published *Contract and Domination*.

57. Mohanty, *Literary Theory and the Claims of History*, 209, 198, xii.

58. See Moya, *Learning from Experience*, 100–35.

59. Mohanty, *Literary Theory and the Claims of History*, 207.

2. DESIRE
The chapter title quote is from Stuart Hall, "What Is This 'Black' in Black Popular Culture?," 467.

1. Appiah, "Racisms," 11.

2. Levinas, *Meaning and Sense*, 52.

3. Rachel Moran notes that "Americans overwhelmingly believe that so long as people do not despise members of another race, they are free to love members of their own race without legal interference or moral reproach" (*Interracial Dating*, 124–25).

4. M. Jacqui Alexander tenders the following political landscape: "Erotic auton-

omy signals danger to the heterosexual family and to the nation. And because loyalty to the nation as citizen is perennially colonized within reproduction and heterosexuality, erotic autonomy brings with it the potential of undoing the nation entirely. . . . Given the putative impulse of this eroticism to corrupt, it signals danger to respectability . . . most significantly to black middle-class womanhood" (*Pedagogies of Crossing*, 22–23). Alexander's chapter "Erotic Autonomy as a Politics of Decolonization: Feminism, Tourism, and the State in the Bahamas" was originally published in 1997 as "Erotic Autonomy as a Politics of Decolonization: An Anatomy of Feminist and State Practice in the Bahamas Tourist Economy." Her work demonstrates the way in which queer erotic autonomy becomes par for the course in theorizing about sexuality and thus represents another strand of (black) queer feminism in line with Rubin's earlier call to think *sex* through erotic autonomy. For Alexander, erotic autonomy undermines the social contract upon which civil engagement is formed—but if one were to think of that contract, as per Charles Mills, as always already predicated upon a profound racial exclusion, then the boundary of erotic autonomy shifts from a choice *outside* the bounds of civil life to a mechanism intrinsic to civil life's apportioning of citizenship and belonging. The problem posed here echoes Marlon Ross's quibble with Robyn Wiegman's work (see note 49 for chapter 1).

5. In her reading of Pat Califia's classic *Macho Sluts*, Linda Hart notes that Califia "implies that a yearning for an absolute is constitutive of sexual desire" (*Between the Body and the Flesh*, 82). Hart's work on lesbian s/m attempts to create a place for the visibility of lesbian desire in a psychoanalysis that renders her manifestation as impossible.

6. Ross, "White Fantasies of Desire," 32.

7. Hames-García, "Can Queer Theory Be Critical Theory?," 216.

8. Freeman, "Time Binds, or, Erotohistoriography," 59. Freeman begins this search for an erotic life in an earlier article coauthored with Lauren Berlant, "Queer Nationality," where they identify the necessity for "an expanded politics of *erotic* description" in the area of the public and the private (154).

9. See Edelman's *No Future*. While Edelman's journey is psychoanalytically driven, there is another discourse on this idea of the future and its *masculinity* in Beauvoir. As she writes: "Man's project is not to repeat himself in time: it is to reign over the instant and to forge the future. Male activity, creating values, has constituted existence itself as value; it has prevailed over the indistinct forces of life; and it has subjugated Nature and Woman" (*The Second Sex*, 77). While we don't talk like that anymore, to echo the *New York Times* review of the new translation, it is important to think about how queer theory's relative obsession with psychoanalysis has prevented critics from taking on some of the finer points about gender and difference it might have inherited from very early French feminisms.

10. While Donald Morton's focus is not on race or racism, in "Birth of the

Cyberqueer" he provides a reading of "desire" and the emergence of queer theory over and against a lesbian and gay studies approach. In thinking through calls by early queer theory to free sexuality from the sphere of regulation and control, Morton notes that Eve Sedgwick's *Epistemology of the Closet* produces a "new space, [where] desire is regarded as autonomous—unregulated and unencumbered" (370). He then notes that his own work "acknowledges the significance of desire but insists on relating desire to the historical world (not an ideal one) and to worldly materiality" (371). Like Rosemary Hennessey, Morton is a firm believer in historical materialism. While I can understand the materialist resistance to a decontextualized postmodern subject, I do wonder what kind of embodiment the subject of Morton's (and for that matter Hennessey's) prose might have. Nevertheless, since Hennessey's important study, other materialist scholars have continued to think through the uncomfortable opposition between queer studies and in particular, Marxist thought. See Judith Butler, "Merely Cultural," and Kevin Floyd, *The Reification of Desire*.

11. Hennessey, *Profit and Pleasure*, 185–86.

12. Hart, *Between the Body and the Flesh*, 59–60.

13. I borrow the phrase from Robert Gooding-Williams's explication of *Casablanca* in "Black Cupids, White Desires," from *Look, A Negro!*, 21. See also work by Lorraine O'Grady, especially "Olympia's Maid" and "Nefertiti/Devonia Evangeline"; along with Wilson, *Lorraine O'Grady*; and Aukeman, "Review of Exhibitions." See also Mullen, *Sleeping with the Dictionary*, *Muse & Drudge*, *S*PeRMK*T*, and *Tree Tall Woman*.

14. Simone de Beauvoir in her musings about the work of Heidegger, Sartre, and Merleau-Ponty concludes that "if the body is not a *thing*, it is a situation: it is our grasp on the world and the outline for our projects" (*The Second Sex*, 46). Work on thing theory can be seen in Moten, "The Case for Blackness." See Spillers, " 'All the Things You Could Be by Now, if Sigmund Freud's Wife Was Your Mother' " in *Black, White, and in Color*.

15. For a superb redaction of important feminist work on Simone de Beauvoir, see Sonia Kruks, "Beauvoir's Time/Our Time." Margaret Simons in particular attempts to deal with the three issues stated here; see her *Beauvoir and "The Second Sex."* Beauvoir was the subject of one of Judith Butler's early essays, "Sex and Gender in Simone de Beauvoir's *The Second Sex*," and other early essays point to the fact that Butler was a key player in feminist philosophical interpretations of Beauvoir's legacy. Toril Moi's essay "While We Wait" specifically notes that one of Butler's exceptions to Beauvoir is actually due to faulty translation. Moi observes: "Apart from the fact that I can't quite see why it's normative to say that the body is a situation, the 'instrumentality' invoked by Butler [in *Gender Trouble*] is clearly Parshley's" (1023).

16. Beauvoir, *The Second Sex*, 416, 67. In the Parshley volume the second quote is

translated as: "Eroticism implies a claim of the instant against time, the individual against the group; . . . it is rebellion against all regulation; it contains a principle hostile to society" (212; Simone de Beauvoir, *The Second Sex*, translated by H. M. Parshley [1952]). I juxtapose this Parshley translation and the new translation to note the difference between the two, and the fact that faulty translation can lead to misreadings of Beauvoir's intention. In essence both Margaret Simons in "The Silencing of Simone de Beauvoir" and Toril Moi in "While We Wait" have demonstrated that the Parshley translation is inadequate. Further, in Moi's words, by "completely betraying Beauvoir's thought, the English text leads Anglophone feminist philosophers into error. The effect is to diminish the feminist intellectual enterprise as a whole" (1023). See also Sarah Glazer, "Lost in Translation," *New York Times*, August 22, 2004. After struggles with Knopf (the original publisher of the Parshley translation) and Gallimard—a struggle noted in some detail by Moi—*The Second Sex* was published in England in December 2009 and in the United States in April 2010. Despite the anticipation among Americanists working in the United States academy, Francine du Plessix Gray's "Dispatches from the Other: A New Translation of *The Second Sex*" (*New York Times*, May 30, 2010), a review of the new translation, is less than favorable. She notes: "Should we rejoice that this first unabridged edition of 'The Second Sex' appears in a new translation? I, for one, do not. Executed by two American women who have lived in Paris for many years and taught English at the Institut de'Études Politiques, it doesn't begin to flow as nicely as Parshley's."

17. I run the risk of moving against Deborah Bergoffen's sense that "autonomy," at least in *The Ethics of Ambiguity*, "may be the ground value of the I, but it also directs us to the value of the other and requires that the I be responsive to the demands of the we" ("Out from Under," 185; see also her *The Philosophy of Simone de Beauvoir*). In essence, some queer theory interpretations of autonomy have been in large part irresponsible ones, demonstrated in a kind of libertine ethic. There is little sense that the demands of the "we" help motivate the intentions of this queer citizenry. Ironically enough, Simone de Beauvoir's tract on the Marquis de Sade, *Must We Burn de Sade?*, establishes both the importance of his philosophical intervention and the terms in which we must repudiate his conclusions for ethical reasons.

18. My question here parallels, and runs into deep contradiction with, the marking of the project at hand by one black feminist: "A queer black feminist practice requires marking race and class in relation to desire and reveals that the telling of desire must always be a text written about race and class no matter how encoded within gender oppression" (Harris, "Queer Black Feminism," 12). The issue here is not with the desire to make race matter, but how that intellectual possibility is mired in a material requirement that black somehow equals or speaks to race in

exclusion of all other subjectivities and identities that can also speak to the matter at hand.

19. The development of Beauvoir's argument is in part a response to the overt sexism of some philosophical inquiry. In particular, as Richard Cohen notes, Beauvoir took it upon herself to level the accusation of "sexism" against Emmanuel Levinas's conceptualization of women's sex in his *Time and the Other*. Although Cohen, along with other critics that he points us toward, wants to believe that Beauvior judged Levinas too harshly, the section that follows "Eros"—"Fecundity"—has a take on "paternity" (91) that still privileges *inheritance* (biological or psychological) as a property or function of the male. Levinas's presence in the work of queer studies is most deeply felt in Judith Butler's work (notably *Undoing Gender, Precarious Life,* and *Gender Trouble*), and given his focus on "death, sexuality, paternity" in *Time and the Other* (92), it is easy to see why, although I do sometimes wonder what more or less does Levinas have to offer queer studies on this subject than Beauvoir. Nevertheless, it is hard not to see the value of Levinas's critique of the ego in relationship to the three categories, as for Levinas, "sexuality, paternity, and death introduce a duality to existence, a duality that concerns the very existing of each subject" (92). Regardless, for Levinas sexuality is something that cannot be accomplished without relation with *another*—it requires *connection*.

20. Lorde, "Uses of the Erotic," 54.

21. Ibid., 55. While feminists have utilized Lorde's work somewhat, little attention as been paid to it in feminist *theory* as a whole. It is interesting to note that the editor of *Sister Outsider*, Nancy Bereano, thought of both the collection and Lorde's work as *theoretical*. As she noted, "There can be no doubt that *Sister Outsider*, a collection of essays and speeches drawn from the past eight years of this Black lesbian feminist's nonfiction prose, makes absolutely clear to many what some already knew: Audre Lorde's voice is central to the development of contemporary feminist theory. She is at the cutting edge of consciousness" (7). I find the use of the word "consciousness" to be an allusion to feminist philosophy, and to the Beauvoir legacy in particular—a point that might have been missed in most utilizations of Lorde's oeuvre.

22. See Ahmed, *Queer Phenomenology*. Ahmed wants to rethink the term "orientation" and its relationship to "the spatiality of sexuality, gender and race" (2). Most importantly she wants queer studies to be in "closer dialogue" with phenomenology (1). She also reads across several epistemological registers including critical race theory, thus making this one of the few queer studies projects to acknowledge its debt to that branch of critical thought. Ahmed's book does repeat the feminist tendency to treat "race" and "sexuality" as rather discrete categories by separating her analysis of them into two chapters ("Sexual Orientation" and "The Orient and Other Others," respectively). In addition, Randall Halle's *Queer Social Philosophy*

seeks to undo the victim status of the term "queer," and the group, in relationship to heterosexuality. By retelling the story of queer's rise as a term in social philosophy, Halle hopes to retool our understanding of "queer" as necessarily oppositional. Halle's analysis of Kant reiterates his articulation of the categorical imperative as "the means whereby will as a generalizing act of reason moves individuals from acts based on their particular dispositions [sexual acts/lust] to acts of communal interest" (55). For my purposes here, queer serves to remind the heteronormative that certain persons commit certain acts for individual pleasure and not the greater good, and therefore these individuals are a threat to civil society. This is precisely the social irresponsibility that Halle attempts to disrupt.

23. In Prosser's thoroughgoing analysis of Butler's contributions to lesbian, gay, bisexual, and transgender theory, he identifies Butler's theoretical misstep in a misinterpretation of Freud that then "reconfigures sex from material corporeality into phantasized surface" (*Second Skins*, 40). See in particular chapter 1, "Judith Butler: Queer Feminism, Transgender, and the Transsubstantiation of Sex."

24. Ahmed, *Queer Phenomenology*, 118.

25. This query has its mirror in Robert Reid-Pharr's observation of Melvin Van Peebles's filmography: "The difficulty faced by the midcentury Black American intellectual was the recognition that, the power of the erotic being what it is, supposed black and white combatants might indeed have become so intimate by early 1970s that it was difficult, if not impossible to see where black innocence began and white guilt ended" (*Once You Go Black*, 165).

26. In Butler's concluding chapter of *Gender Trouble*, she remarks: "I began with a speculative question of whether feminist politics could do without a 'subject' in the category of women. At stake is not whether it still makes sense, strategically or transitionally, to refer to women in order to make representational claims in their behalf. The feminist 'we' is always and only a phantasmatic construction, one that has its purposes, but which denies the internal complexity and indeterminacy of the term and constitutes itself only through the exclusion of some part of the constituency that it simultaneously seeks to represent" (142). The investment in the "subjectless" critique manifests itself most vividly in the work of Kandice Chuh's *Imagine Otherwise*, although that work is not focused upon the category of women, as such.

27. Butler, *Gender Trouble*, 152 n. 15.

28. See Heinämaa, *Toward a Phenomenology of Sexual Difference*. For another feminist reassessment of Beauvoir's legacy, see Moi, *Simone de Beauvoir*, especially her comparison between Beauvoir and Fanon, in chapter 7, "Beauvoir's Utopia: The Politics of *The Second Sex*."

29. Heinämaa, *Toward a Phenomenology of Sexual Difference*, 75. See also Merleau-Ponty, *The Phenomenology of Perception*, especially the chapter "The Body in Its Sexual Being."

30. Nancy Bauer traces the usefulness of the Hegelian dialectic of master/slave to Beauvoir in *Simone de Beauvoir, Philosophy, and Feminism*.

31. Given the importance of Lorde's statement to feminism at the time, it is interesting that in Lynda Hart's work on lesbian s/m (*Between the Body and the Flesh*) and liberal feminism's penchant for representing lesbian sex as sanitized and full of feeling, she chose not to launch a critique of Lorde's positing of the erotic in contradistinction to the pornographic.

32. Nash, "Strange Bedfellows," 52. Nash proposes that "in place of a normative reading of racialized pornography, [my theory of] racial iconography asks new questions about black spectatorship and black visual pleasures, attending to the historical and technological specificity of both. In doing so, racial iconography allows black feminists to break with a lengthy tradition of sexual conservatism and to instead embark on what Evelynn Hammonds has called a 'politics of articulation'" (69). Moreover, one could see how nicely Nash's observation of black pleasure and spectatorship changes the alignment of racist practice from something that white subjects do to black subjects to a more complicated playing field where erotic *autonomy* might have more traction.

33. This staged opposition between black feminism and queer studies has also been explored by Laura Alexandra Harris in "Queer Black Feminism: The Pleasure Principle." She observes: "Black feminist theory is likewise in turmoil over its parameters, its institutional position, and grapples with the theorizing of sexuality. Revealingly, it only occasionally finds itself articulated in relation to the overdetermining queer and feminist paradigms. . . . The dominant academic exclusion of black feminism as 'other' discourse, not queer not feminist, has a history both far-reaching and contemporary" (5).

34. Rubin's essay sees its subject as a sexual minority hounded and at times ravaged by a system of "sex law." Her goal is to move feminist discourse away from the stance of those such as Women Against Pornography that often colludes with the state and its policing force. About her essay she states the following: "In the last six years, new erotic communities, political alliances, and analyses have been developed in the midst of the repression. . . . [I] propose elements of a descriptive and conceptual framework for thinking about sex and its politics [and] I hope to contribute to the pressing task of creating an accurate, human, and genuinely liberatory body of thought about sexuality" ("Thinking Sex," 275). She also notes that a "democractic morality should judge sexual acts by the way partners treat one another, the level of mutual consideration, the presence or absence of coercion, and the quantity and quality of the pleasures they provide. Whether sex acts are gay or straight, coupled or in groups, naked or in underwear, commercial or free, with or without video, should not be ethical concerns" (283). While Rubin's call does seem to be liberatory, the worry for feminist theorists should be what then does count as "ethical"?

35. Walker, "A Letter of the Times, Or Should This Sado-Masochism Be Saved?," 207.

36. In the essay "The Politics of Sado-Masochistic Fantasies," Robin Morgan reiterates feminist takes on historical attachments. As she notes, "There are, to be sure, various books recently published on the fantasy lives of women. These books range from the pseudoscientific to the soft-core-porn in their approach. Here we can encounter the virulently anti-feminist thought of such Freudians as Marie Robinson, whose book *The Power of Sexual Surrender* is to women what a tome called *Why You Know You Love It on the Plantation* would be to blacks or one titled *How to Be Happy in Line to the Showers* would be to Jews" (109). When histories line up nicely and attach themselves to their objects, the chance for meaningful exchange diminishes. Making political points via analogy has plagued the Left since the new vangardism of the late 1950s and early 1960s. The most recent incarnation would be in the "like race" arguments for gay marriage. See Halley, " 'Like Race' Arguments."

37. Although Diane Harriford, who currently blogs for *Ms.* magazine, was present at the conference and gave a paper titled "Sexual Purity: Maintaining Class and Race Boundaries" at the Barnard conference, her paper did not make the publication of *Pleasure and Danger*. In addition, Olivia Espín contributed a paper, "Cultural and Historical Influences on Sexuality in Hispanic/Latin Women: Implications for Psychotherapy," to both the conference and the volume, but her work deals mostly with the relationship of Latinas within "Latin" culture. Hortense Spillers is one of the only conference participants to deal head on with the issue of the black/white binary in feminism: "Black American women in the public/critical discourse of feminist thought have not acknowledged sexuality because they enter the historical stage from quite another angle of entrance than that of Anglo-American women. Even though my remarks are addressed specifically to feminists, I do not doubt that the different historical occasions implicated here have dictated sharp patterns of divergence not only in living styles, but also ways of speaking between black and white American women, without modification. We must have refinement in the picture at the same time that we recognize that *history* has divided the empire of women against itself. As a result, black American women project in their thinking about the female circumstance and their own discourse concerning it an apparently divergent view from feminist thinking on the issues. I am not comfortable with the 'black-woman/feminist' opposition that this argument apparently cannot avoid. I am also not cheered by what seems a little noticed elision of meaning—when we say 'feminist' without an adjective in front of it, we mean, of course, white women, who, as a category of social and cultural agents, fully occupy the territory of feminism" ("Interstices," 79). In this book I return to this early feminist concern about history and black/white bodies, with the aim of correcting the idea of separate but equal that the first sentence of Spillers's quote seems to imply.

38. In chapter 1 of *The Trouble with Normal* Warner says it is "moralism" rather than "morality" when certain tastes or sex practices are mandated for everyone. Suspicion of sexual variance among those who think their own way of living is right "is pseudo-morality, the opposite of an ethical respect for the autonomy of others" (4). A respect for the autonomy of others is itself a moral argument that works against violence toward "women, sissies, and variant sexualities" (5). Furthermore, having an ethic of sex, Warner argues, does not mean having a theory about what peoples' desires should and should not be. In noting that the potential for abject shame always accompanies sex, Warner observes that the ethical vision within queer circles is precisely that one "doesn't pretend to be *above* the indignity of sex . . . A relation to others, in these contexts, begins in an acknowledgement of all that is most abject and least reputable in oneself. Shame is bedrock. Queers can be abusive, insulting, and vile toward one another, but because abjection is understood to be the shared condition, they also know how to communicate through such camaraderie a moving and unexpected form of generosity . . . The rule is: Get over yourself" (35). The question here is whether or not the same ethical standard extends to the racial. This problem is addressed in the opening to my second chapter where the play of ethical commitment and racialized desire are evident.

39. For example, see the posting on the blog Racialicious by Andrea Plaid, "I Like the Erotic and the Porn: Looking Back at Audre Lorde's 'Uses of the Erotic,' " July 9, 2009, www.racialicious.com.

40. Lorde, "Uses of the Erotic," 56.

41. Marlon Ross also points out the importance of "non(re)production" in his discussion of the heightened visibility in cities in the United States of "out" homosexuals: "White urbane homosexuality maneuvers between, on the one hand, a respectable high society in need of homosexuals as a sign of the right to nonproductive luxury and, on the other hand, the unrespectable margins of forbidden, self-destructive criminality" ("Camping the Dirty Dozens," 297).

42. Martin, "Sexualities without Genders and Other Queer Utopias," 107.

43. In Martin's analysis of Sedgwick's explication of the relationship between sex, gender, and sexuality, she states: "The result is that lesbians, or women in general, become interesting by making a cross-gender identification or an identification with sexuality, now implicitly (though, I think, not intentionally) associated with men, over against gender and by extension, feminism and women" ("Sexualities without Genders and Other Queer Utopias," 107). In addition, Laura Alexandra Harris notes: "Queer, as it is often claimed by academically powerful white masculinity, sometimes suggests and describes its political constituency as seductively fluid, unmarked, ambiguous, and chosen. This fluidity sounds dangerously like the status of white masculinity to me" ("Queer Black Feminism," 12).

44. Kruks, "Beauvoir's Time/Our Time," 306.

45. See Firestone, *The Dialectic of Sex*. Firestone's claim that technology (the pill,

for example) would ultimately free women of their bodies is one of the most forward-thinking pronouncements in the early canon. It is my contention that later work from posthuman and cyborg feminism (N. Katherine Hayles and Donna Haraway among others) stems from this early work.

46. Quoted in Halle, *Queer Social Philosophy*, 114. See also D'Emilio, "Capitalism and Gay Identity."

47. This chapter's conclusions about the erotic read against my earlier thoughts on Lorde's work. See my essay "To Touch the Mother's C[o]untry," especially page 220.

48. Butler, *Antigone's Claim*, 23. Michael Cobb also uses Butler's argument in *Antigone's Claim* to think through the place of incest in public narratives of homophobia. He finds that "the horror of incest is the current way to mark, to figure, the limits of what kinds of sexual tolerance toward gays, lesbians, and bisexuals the current, extremely conservative political climate can accommodate" ("Race, Religion, Hate and Incest in Queer Politics," 259). Although Cobb's essay is concerned with "like race" arguments, his attention to the incest taboo doesn't necessarily rethink its particular place in the spectrum of American social life that I have outlined here.

49. Again, this could be queer theory's inheritance from phenomenological reconceptualizations of "time" (as in Beauvoir's earlier statement) and the relationship of time to the intentionality of human being. Interestingly, Deborah Bergoffen's work on Beauvoir attempts to mark Beauvoir's departure from Sartre's conceptualization of intention, disclosure, freedom, and bad faith by recognizing her introduction of delight and desire to the matrix of consciousness. In doing so, Bergoffen focuses on the place of the child in existential work (*Being and Nothingness* and *The Ethics of Ambiguity*). She notes: "Not only does she identify the child as innocent, that is, as not being in bad faith, she also identifies others, 'the negro slave of the 18th century' and 'the Mohammedan woman enclosed in a harem' who exist in situations that preclude their knowing their freedom and whose submission to the authority of the other cannot be counted as an act of bad faith" ("Out from Under," 183). Bergoffen takes no issue with Beauvoir's relegation of "Mohammedan" subjectivity to the sphere of the child and its lack of personal agency in the face of the desire of another. The "harem" (whatever that might be in Beauvoir's mind) experience might not be an *acquiescence* to domination but rather a thorough understanding of the place of the *hegemonic* (in the Gramscian sense) in human relations.

50. Halperin, "Is There a History of Sexuality?," 259 (emphasis mine). Halperin's argument here is to consider the place of sex among the ancients. In this community of citizens and others, Halperin finds that sex was something to be performed on subordinates by superordinates and it therefore indicated social status rather than dictating a particular ontology.

51. Ibid., 259, 271.

52. This reading is supported by Marlon Ross's accounting of the emergence of the homosexual in "Beyond the Closet as Raceless Paradigm." Ross also makes reference to Siobhan Somerville's contention in "Scientific Racism and the Emergence of the Homosexual Body." Work on the connection between race, sex, sexuality, and sexual practice in the nineteenth century can also be attributed to the scholarly contributions of Sander Gilman, especially "Black Bodies, White Bodies."

3. S.H.E.

1. Faukner, *Light in August*, 487.

2. The most extended critique of subjectlessness in Butler's *Gender Trouble* can be found in Paula Moya's *Learning from Experience*. Moya argues quite persuasively that it is Butler's misreading of Cherríe Moraga and jettisoning of a certain kind of French feminism that "clears the way for her to do away with the category of 'woman' altogether" (34).

3. Elizabeth Weed, "The More Things Change," 250.

4. Rosi Braidotti with Judith Butler, "Feminism by Any Other Name," 31.

5. There is the overarching feeling that Butler's third book, *Bodies That Matter*, with its readings of *Paris Is Burning* and *Passing* was an attempt to respond to the psychic life of such criticism by producing readings that would attend to those bodies in some direct way. But I believe that Hammond's initial critique here is invaluable—the call was never to speak to the woman of color as subject, but to *subject* a thoroughgoing critique of the category to the discursive importance of racism's *work* in the field of inquiry. But in Butler's defense, how could she not have made such a pedestrian mistake about the call here, as so many of the interlocutors at conferences across the country were calling for attention to specific bodies, rather than a discursive field of investigation.

6. The clear exception here is Carole-Anne Tyler's "Passing: Narcissism, Identity and Difference," where she engages the place of psychoanalysis within feminist/ queer theorizing. Tyler notes that "gender is often in danger of being ignored as a significant difference within theories and activisms which seek to construct a community of adherents who share identities and a commitment to a single 'master signifier'—whether it is class, race, or sexuality—as that which can explain everything (the inverse is also true, and in recent years feminism has focused intensively on 'differences within')" (233). Tyler points to the problem of the "master signifier" in emerging queer theory as the cure-all for a persistent forgetting. It is a shame that her stunning monograph *Female Impersonation* was published after *Gender Trouble*, as her concerted readings in that text really do much to take into consideration some of the larger concerns of feminism and queer theory while not totally forgetting the awkward and sometimes unmanageable materiality of the body altogether (see especially the chapter "Feminism, Racism and Impersonation").

7. Hammonds, "Black (W)holes and the Geometry of Black Female Sexuality," 127 (emphasis in original).

8. For work in queer native studies, see GLQ: A Gay and Lesbian Quarterly, "Sexuality, Nationality, Indigeneity." In the time between the publication of the *differences* special issue and the "Plum Nelly" special issue of *Callaloo*, a special issue of *Social Text* was published titled "Queer Transexions of Race, Nation, and Gender." This special issue consists of a wide range of contributors, many of them outside the field of queer studies. The editors (Phillip Brian Harper, Anne McClintock, José Esteban Muñoz, and Trish Rosen) note that theirs is a " 'queer' critique, conceived as a means of traversing and creatively transforming conceptual boundaries, thereby harnessing the critical potential of queer theory while deploying it beyond the realms of sexuality and sexual identity" (1). I am not including a review of the essays in this collection, although its appearance is timely because the authors do not necessarily set themselves in opposition to or conceive of their project as a critique of a prevailing queer theory, although they do conceive of the volume as an "intervention."

9. See chapter 5 of my *Raising the Dead*, where I speak to the presence of the angry black lesbian in feminist discourse.

10. Muñoz, *Disidentifications*, 6. Jason King thanks Muñoz specifically for contributing to the ideas in his essay "Any Love: Silence, Theft, and Rumor in the Work of Luther Vandross" (443), indicating there was a fair amount of connectivity between the *Black Queer Studies* project and an emerging queer of color critique.

11. I do not think so, although certainly in my experience in academia I have encountered my share of queer prejudice—at Stanford it came in the form of a slip of the tongue. One of my senior colleagues actually managed to call Condoleezza Rice (then provost) the "n" word during one of his lectures. Unfortunately, folks were too invested in hating Rice (locally and globally) to invest any political capital in protesting such an outrage, and since Rice said nothing publicly about the matter, the incident gained no political traction or national attention.

12. This moment does bring us back to the beginnings of *radical* feminism, as early second wave feminists joined with black women in their critique of the sexism in the civil rights struggle. See Echols, *Daring to Be Bad*. It is still one of the only texts to take a full accounting of radical feminist organizations that emerged in the late 1960s and early 1970s and an effort to assess their importance to an emerging second wave of feminism.

13. See Henderson, "James Baldwin," 320.

14. As for the particularity of the black body, I am in no way arguing that this marginalization is the fault of "white" critics. Anyone alive and breathing during the culture wars of the 1980s—a time when I was finishing college and entering graduate school—knows that the often misguided lingua franca of affirmative ac-

tion on college and university campuses caused identity-bound groups to think of themselves through a kind of strategic essentialism (after Spivak)—a posture that might have been politically advantageous in the short run, but in the long run has had devastating consequences for public policy and university life. The critical race legal scholar Richard Thompson Ford in his analysis in *Racial Culture* brilliantly outlines what some of these consequences have been, at least in the legal arena.

15. It would be intellectually dishonest if I did not report that Nada Elia's " 'A Man Who Wants To Be a Woman?' " actually resists this neat narrative, as she establishes "queer theory" as the "consequence of such movements as poststructuralism and postcolonialism, which first successfully challenged and critiqued, as they sought to overcome, oppressive binary polarities" (353). Theory is the thing that comes *after* other movements and is therefore released from its responsibility to speak to or for another.

16. It is generally thought that the idea of the transnational comes out of a post-9/11 reality, shored up by the ongoing discourse of postcoloniality. Ann duCille critiques the relationship among African American studies, Afrocentricity, and postcoloniality in *Skin Trade*. She concludes: "If we could see beyond the tufts of straw and the feet of clay, I wonder what practitioners of these three discourses . . . might learn from one another, and in particular what we might teach one another about the white academy that both claims and disclaims us" (135). DuCille's point is an important one, though it has no circulation among black queer studies critics. Although duCille worries about the relationship among the three fields, ironically enough she would later go on to help found a journal in transnational studies, *Diaspora: A Journal of Transnational Studies*.

17. Harper's *Callaloo* piece is actually an expanded reprint of an essay by the same title published in *Private Affairs: Critical Ventures in the Culture of Social Relations*. It is interesting to note that Harper's piece includes a personal vignette about a train encounter with a gentleman who mistakes him for a Sri Lankan. M. Jacqui Alexander's chapter 2 of "Imperial Desire/Sexual Utopias: White Gay Capital and Transnational Tourism" from *Pedagogies* also includes a selection from Shyam Selvadurai's novel *Funny Boy*, also set in Sri Lanka.

18. I would also like to note that in chapter 4 ("Discourse and Dat Course: Postcoloniality and Afrocentricity") of *Skin Trade*, Ann duCille launches one of the few critiques of the influence of postcolonial thought on a nascent African Americanist project. DuCille sketches the debate between so-called Afrocentrist scholars like Molefi Kete Asante and black intellectuals like Henry Louis Gates, and the relationship between postcolonial studies and Afrocentricity. "What does it mean," she asks, "when Afrocentricity is dismissed as methodologically sloppy, anti-intellectual identity politics, while postcoloniality is affirmed as theoretically sophisticated oppositional discourse?" (123). Although she points out that the des-

ignation "postcolonial" might be relatively new, the study of black power relations between colonizer and colonized has a longer history in the United States (and abroad) among black intellectuals, activists, and scholars. The distinction between these theorists and the Asian scholars associated with postcolonial studies, says duCille, has led to the accusation—from some Afrocentrists—that "foreigners" are once again taking over the field and that the interest of outsiders was needed to "legitimize a discourse of which the academy took little note when it was dominated by diasporic blacks" (125). But duCille stresses that postcolonial studies is not just a beneficiary of or heir to other resistance narratives but is indeed its own reaction to the oppressions of imperialism. If Afrocentricity has restricted its critique of hegemonic systems to its own local politics, she says, postcoloniality, because of its engagement with theories of difference, has the potential to present such a critique on a global level. DuCille cautions against appropriations of postcolonial status to reaffirm the European or Anglo-American center, however, and stresses the importance of strategic essentialism: "What I would wish for postcolonialism . . . is not the therapeutic essentialism of Afrocentricity but the strategic essentialism of an interculturally orientated African American studies" (134). She ends the chapter with the assertion that the three discourses—African American studies, postcoloniality, and Afrocentricity—all have something to "teach one another about the white academy that both claims and disclaims us" (135). On the transnational and Anzaldúa's work, see also Debra A. Castillo, "Anzaldua and Transnational American Studies." Castillo attempts to think through Anzaldúa's legacy among her detractors and her critical allies.

19. Harper, " 'Take Me Home,' " 464; emphasis in original.

20. Ibid., 476.

21. Robert Reid-Pharr, inherently on the outside of this black queer studies endeavor and suspicious of its *naming* at least, suggests "that it is not nearly so easy as presumably it once was to establish with anything approaching certainty the essence of either a queer or a black subjectivity" (*Once You Go Black*, 147).

22. Johnson and Henderson, *Black Queer Studies*, 3; emphasis mine.

23. Walcott, "Outside in Black Studies," 92.

24. Johnson, " 'Quare' Studies," 129; emphasis in original.

25. Ross, "Beyond the Closet as Raceless Paradigm," 162.

26. *Black Queer Studies* was the result of a paradigm-shifting conference, "Black Queer Studies in the Millennium" (2000), organized by Henderson and Johnson at the University of North Carolina (UNC). Although *Aberrations* appeared *before* the publication of the *Black Queer Studies* volume, much of the content of the collection had been circulating widely in the critical community as a result of the UNC conference. See also Dwight McBride's assessment of its importance in his chapter "Straight Black Studies," in *Why I Hate Abercrombie & Fitch: Essays on Race and Sexuality*.

27. Ferguson later argues: "African American culture, as this book has attempted to illustrate, functions as one location that negates and critiques the normative itineraries of capitalist modes of production" (137). This is quite a tall order for African American culture—that of making it the arbiter of a wide range of goings on in the community at large. Ferguson attempts to parse this statement in his conclusion by utilizing Cathy Cohen's work on the new place of the black middle class as the "overseer of queer, poor, HIV-positive, and drug-addicted persons in black communities, becoming the normative antithesis to deviant African American subjects" (145). This parsing places black middle-class identities within larger structures of control and domination.

28. M. Jacqui Alexander in *Pedagogies* (23–24) attributes the founding of this term to the work of Lynda Hart, *Fatal Women*.

29. See Spillers, "Interstices," 76.

30. It is also important to mark that Roderick Ferguson and Michael Cobb are the only "Plum Nelly" and *Black Queer Studies* contributors who appear in the "What's Queer about Queer Studies Now" special issue.

31. Puar, *Terrorist Assemblages*, 24.

32. This is a queer liberalism that gets marked as "white" in Hiram Perez's essay "You Can Have My Brown Body and Eat It, Too!" As Perez notes, "I speculate in this essay on the resistance within establishmentarian queer theory to thinking race critically, a resistance that habitually classifies almost any form of race studies as a retreat into identity politics. This defensive posture helps entrench institutionally the transparent white subject characteristic of so much queer theorizing. Queer theorists who can invoke that transparent subject, and choose to do so, reap the dividends of whiteness" (171). Perez notes that his theory of whiteness is taken from a well-known critical race essay by Cheryl Harris, "Whiteness as Property." In addition, Judith Halberstam's essay "Shame and White Gay Masculinity" references the same conference that Perez interrogates (Gay Shame, University of Michigan, March 27–29, 2003) and explicitly names white gay male homonormativity as the problem that queer of color critique seeks to engage. It is here that Jacqui Alexander's work gets a mention, but it is not her monograph. Instead it is the collection Alexander edited with Chandra Talpade Mohanty, *Feminist Genealogies, Colonial Legacies, Democratic Futures*.

33. Alexander, *Pedagogies of Crossing*, 70.

34. I can think of three black feminist contributions that have been important to debates about sexuality, belonging, citizenship, and race: Cohen, *The Boundaries of Blackness*; Holland, *Raising the Dead*; and Alexander, *Pedagogies of Crossing*. The publication dates for *Pedagogies* and the *Social Text* special issue are the same, but the omission of Alexander's work is puzzling because it comes out of Halberstam's series at Duke, so at least one of the editors would have been aware of Alexander's intervention. This could be due to the fact that Alexander's book is a collection of

essays—many of the key ones were published in the late 1990s. In particular, Alexander frames her project as "an inventory of sorts of my multifaceted journey with(in) feminism, an inventory that is necessarily pluralized by virtue of my own migrations and the confluence of different geographies of feminism. In this volume I am concerned with the multiple operations of power, of gendered and sexualized power that is simultaneously raced and classed yet not practiced within hermetically sealed or epistemically partial borders of the nation-state" (4). Perhaps it is Alexander's relationship to an always already jettisoned feminism that prevents her work from being engaged with in this round of queer studies critique? To this list I would also add Hortense Spillers, *Black, White, and in Color*. That the powerhouse presses for queer studies work are Duke University, New York University, and the University of Minnesota cannot be argued, given the concentration of texts from these three publishing houses in the editor's list of influential work. It is interesting to note that two of the texts I mention here are from the University of Chicago Press. One of the most prolific and vocal queer native scholars is Craig Womack, notably his *Red on Red*.

35. See duCille, "The Occult of True Black Womanhood," 593, 624.

36. Joon Oluchi Lee, "The Joy of the Castrated Boy," 38.

37. See chapter 5 in Holland, *Raising the Dead*.

38. See, among others, Reid-Pharr, Brody, Cohen, Johnson, Trafton, Somerville, Cobb, Spillers, duCille, Harper, Ross, McBride.

39. Cobb, "Race, Religion, Hate and Incest in Queer Politics," 267.

40. Halley notes that Rich's list is derived from a "catalogue of the eight characteristics of male power propounded by Kathleen Gough in 1975" (*Split Decisions*, 195), making the series of lists seem to collapse upon one another and marking the referential in this case as rather impossible.

CONCLUSION

1. See Gilroy, *Against Race*; Appiah and Gates Jr., *Identities*; and Michaels, *Our America*.

2. Toni Morrison, "Home," 6.

3. Derrida was not the last scholar to have at racism. A full decade later, Dinesh D'Souza would publish *The End of Racism*.

4. I want to note that Derrida's essay was published with a lengthy critique by Anne McClintock and Rob Nixon, to which Derrida also responded. In essence, they remind Derrida, as one must rarely remind Morrison and Hurston, that a word's *meaning* is not separate from its *history*, and this relationship gives us a word's politics, forms the epicenter of its nervous system. For Derrida, it is precisely this logic of relation—the idea that history creates meaning rather than confounds it—that causes a word to adhere in one place and experience repudiation in an-

other. I believe that McClintock and Nixon misunderstand Derrida's intent. Derrida doesn't necessarily repudiate racism's checkered history so much as he wants to isolate the word itself and deploy it as a floating signifier, or contaminant. What he finds is that so long as racism is perceived as someone else's problem by those who live in its midst, history cannot adequately account for it. His view is radical in that it emphasizes a lack of responsibility for racism that is epidemic in global cultures.

5. G. M. James Gonzalez in her essay "Of Property: On 'Captive' 'Bodies,' Hidden 'Flesh,' and Colonization" (1997) observes that "tongue (language, voice, rhetoric) and thought (ideology) have been among the deadliest instruments of colonialism. . . . Tongue and thought are, therefore, infectious and untrustworthy within the colonizer and the colonized; for the colonized has also been infected" (129).

6. This conclusion is indebted to the long history of ruminations on the touch in both philosophical and feminist traditions. For other explorations of "touch," see Vasseleu, *Textures of Light*; and Grosz, "Merleau-Ponty and Irigaray in the Flesh."

7. Derrida writes "Le Toucher" as a tribute to the work of his friend and colleague, Jean-Luc Nancy.

8. Kimberlé Crenshaw first used the term "intersectionality" in 1992. Ann duCille utilized "intersection" as a trope in her essay on black women in the academy, "The Occult of True Black Womanhood: Critical Demeanor and Black Feminist Studies" (1994).

9. Quoted in Lippit, *Electric Animal*, 99. Lippit uses this passage to demonstrate Freud's reliance upon the narrative of evolution (borrowed from Darwin) to engage the "estrangement of human beings from subjectivity" (98).

10. Similarly, N. Katherine Hayles explores the role of "virtual bodies" in cyberculture and asks: "What to make of this shift from the human to the posthuman, which both evokes terror and excites pleasure?" (*How We Became Posthuman*, 4).

11. See Derrida's *Le Toucher, Jean-Luc Nancy* (2000). I want to thank Tom Cohen and J. Hillis Miller for bringing this work to my attention.

12. See Derrida's *Of Grammatology* for the protracted discussion of presence/absence.

13. Emily Harris, National Public Radio (NPR), "Study Doubts Jefferson Fathered Hemings' Child," April 13, 2001.

14. Rey Chow explores a parallel project on orientalism as fantasy in her "The Dream of a Butterfly."

15. The romance of Scarlett O'Hara and Rhett Butler is a perfect example of white supremist heterosexual love and has remained the ideal in that portion of the American imaginary where slavery is remembered, if at all.

16. Associated Press, "Jefferson Heirs Plan Cemetery for Slave's Kin," *New York Times*, April 21, 2002.

17. During the course of that tiny interview in a Harvard dormitory, Faulkner

writes that the boundary between the past and the present becomes increasingly porous: "It was not even four now but compounded still further, since now both of them [Quentin and Shreve] were Henry Sutpen and both of them were Bon" (289).

18. See Deleuze and Guattari, *Anti-Oedipus*.

19. I am aware that the change from mother to sister might offer an even more complex snapshot of an incest paradigm in the Americas. Perhaps the bedding of a sister is seen as a lesser charge than the bedding of one's mother—a transgression against biological order itself.

20. Michael Cuesta's award-winning first feature film *L.I.E.* (2000) captures the spirit of what I am arguing here, as one of its secondary characters carries on a relationship with his sister without shame or an acknowledgment of the act of incest.

21. Irving Howe, *William Faulkner*, 118.

22. In telling the story of a New Age woman recounting her past lives to a disinterested partner, Haraway writes the following: "In this cartoon, 'man,' that is Boopsie's bored partner, is the one who listens (sort of) . . . Technology, including the technology of the body itself, is the real subject of universal history. Trudeau knows that the story of technological progress is at the heart of Enlightenment humanism. He also has just the right twist on how the humor works when the subject of technical progress is woman and her body instead of man and his tools" (*Modest_Witness@Second_Millenium.FemaleMan©_Meets_ OncoMouse*, 9). Haraway's explication witnesses the indifference that women's narratives are often greeted with.

23. Fugazi, "Bad Mouth," *13 Days*. The epigraph to this book is reiterated here. The influence of existential thought on Fugazi's music has its mirror in the work of Simone de Beauvoir. At one point in *The Second Sex*, she notes: "For many women, the roads to transcendence are blocked: because they *do* nothing, they do not make themselves *be* anything; they wonder indefinitely what they *could have* become, which leads them to wonder what they *are*: it is a useless questioning; if man fails to find that secret essence, it is simply because it does not exist. Kept at the margins of the world, woman cannot be defined objectively through this world, and her mystery conceals nothing but emptiness" (trans. Constance Borde and Sheila Malovany-Chevallier [New York: Alfred A. Knopf, 2010], 271).

Bibliography

Ahmed, Sara. *Queer Phenomenology: Orientations, Objects, Others*. Durham: Duke University Press, 2006.

Alcoff, Linda. "The Problem of Speaking for Others." *Cultural Critique* 20 (winter 1991–92): 5–32.

Alexander, M. Jacqui. "Erotic Autonomy as a Politics of Decolonization: An Anatomy of Feminist and State Practice in the Bahamas Tourist Economy." In *Feminist Genealogies, Colonial Legacies, Democratic Futures*, edited by M. Jacqui Alexander and Chandra Talpade Mohanty, 63–100. New York: Routledge, 1997.

——. *Pedagogies of Crossing: Meditations on Feminism, Sexual Politics, Memory, and the Sacred*. Durham: Duke University Press, 2005.

Anzaldúa, Gloria. *Borderlands/La Frontera: The New Mestiza*. San Francisco: Aunt Lute, 1987.

Appiah, Kwame Anthony. "Racisms." In *Anatomy of Racism*, edited by David Theo Goldberg, 3–17. Minneapolis: University of Minnesota Press, 1990.

Appiah, Kwame Anthony, and Henry Louis Gates Jr., eds. *Identities*. Chicago: University of Chicago Press, 1995.

Aukeman, Anastasia. "Review of Exhibitions: Lorraine O'Grady." *Art in America* 82, no. 7 (July 1994): 93–94.

Baldwin, James. *The Price of the Ticket: Collected Nonfiction, 1948–1985*. New York: St. Martin's/Marek, 1985.

Barrett, Linden. *Blackness and Value: Seeing Double*. Cambridge: Cambridge University Press, 1999.

Bauer, Nancy. *Simone de Beauvoir, Philosophy, and Feminism*. New York: Columbia University Press, 2001.

Baxendall, Rosalyn. "Re-visioning the Women's Liberation Movement's Narrative: Early Second Wave African American Feminists." *Feminist Studies* 27, no. 1 (spring 2001), 225–45.

Beauvoir, Simone de. *Must We Burn de Sade?* London: P. Nevill, 1953.

———. *The Second Sex*. Translated by Constance Borde and Sheila Malovany-Cheallier. New York: Alfred A. Knopf, 2010.

Bergoffen, Debra B. "Out from Under: Beauvoir's Philosophy of the Erotic." In *Feminist Interpretations of Simone de Beauvoir*, edited by Margaret A. Simons, 179–92. University Park: Pennsylvania State University Press, 1995.

———. *The Philosophy of Simone de Beauvoir: Gendered Phenomenologies, Erotic Generosities*. Albany: State University of New York Press, 1997.

Berlant, Lauren, and Elizabeth Freeman. "Queer Nationality." *boundary 2* 19, no. 1 (spring 1992): 149–80.

Berlant, Lauren, and Michael Warner, "What Does Queer Theory Teach Us about X?" *PMLA* 110, no. 3 (May 1995): 343–49.

Bernasconi, Robert, ed., with Sybol Cook. *Race and Racism in Continental Philosophy*. Bloomington: Indiana University Press, 2003.

Bonilla-Silva, Eduardo. *Racism without Racists: Color-Blind Racism and the Persistence of Racial Inequality in the United States*. 2nd ed. Lanham, Md.: Rowman and Littlefield, 2006.

Braidotti, Rosi, with Judith Butler. "Feminism by Any Other Name." *differences* 6, nos. 2–3 (summer–fall 1994): 27–61.

Brown, Wendy. "The Passion of Michel Foucault." *differences* 5, no. 2 (summer 1993): 140–50.

Brown, Wendy, and Janet Halley, eds. *Left Legalism/Left Critique*. Durham: Duke University Press, 2002.

Butler, Judith. "Against Proper Objects." In "More Gender Trouble: Feminism Meets Queer Theory." Special issue, *differences* 6, nos. 2–3 (summer–fall 1994): 1–26.

———. *Antigone's Claim: Kinship between Life and Death*. New York: Columbia University Press, 2000.

———. "Endangered/Endangering: Schematic Racism and White Paranoia." In *Reading Rodney King, Reading Urban Uprising*, edited by Robert Gooding-Williams, 15–22. New York: Routledge, 1993.

———. *Gender Trouble: Feminism and the Subversion of Identity*. New York: Routledge, 1990.

———. "Lesbian S&M: The Politics of Dis-Illusion." In *Against Sadomasochism: A Radical Feminist Analysis*, edited by Robin Ruth Linden et al., 169–74. East Palo Alto, Calif.: Frog in the Well, 1982.

———. "Merely Cultural." In "Queer Transexions of Race, Nation, and Gender." Special issue, *Social Text* 15, nos. 3–4 (fall–winter 1997): 265–77.

———. "Sex and Gender in Simone de Beauvoir's *The Second Sex*." *Yale French Studies* 72 (1986): 35–49.

Castillo, Debra A. "Anzaldúa and Transnational American Studies." *PMLA* 121, no. 1 (January 2006): 260–65.

Chow, Rey. "The Dream of a Butterfly." In *Human, All Too Human*, edited by Diana Fuss, 61–92. New York: Routledge, 1996.

Chuh, Kandice. *Imagine Otherwise: On Asian Americanist Critique*. Durham: Duke University Press, 2003.

Cobb, Michael. "Insolent Racing, Rough Narrative: The Harlem Renaissance's Impolite Queers." In "Plum Nelly: New Essays in Black Queer Studies." Special issue, *Callaloo* 23, no. 1 (winter 2000): 461–78.

———. "Uncivil Wrongs: Race, Religion, Hate and Incest in Queer Politics." In "What's Queer about Queer Studies Now?" Special issue, *Social Text* 23, nos. 3–4, 84–85 (fall–winter 2005): 251–74.

Cohen, Cathy. *The Boundaries of Blackness: AIDS and the Breakdown of Black Politics*. Chicago: University of Chicago Press, 1999.

———. "Punks, Bulldaggers, and Welfare Queens: The Radical Potential of Queer Politics." *GLQ* 3, no. 4 (1997): 437–65.

Crenshaw, Kimberlé. "Mapping the Margins: Intersectionality, Identity Politics, and Violence against Women of Color." *Stanford Law Review* 43, no. 6 (1991): 1241–99.

Crenshaw, Kimberlé, Neil Gotanda, Gary Peller, and Kendall Thomas, eds. *Critical Race Theory: The Key Writings That Formed the Movement*. New York: New Press, 1995.

Culbert, Jennifer L. "Beyond Intention: A Critique of the 'Normal' Criminal Agency, Responsibility, and Punishment in American Death Penalty Jurisprudence." In *The Killing State: Capital Punishment in Law, Politics, and Culture*, edited by Austin Sarat, 206–25. New York: Oxford University Press, 1999.

Darder, Antonia, and Rodolfo D. Torres. *After Race: Racism after Multiculturalism*. New York: New York University Press, 2004.

Deleuze, Gilles, and Félix Guattari. *Anti-Oedipus: Capitalism and Schizophrenia*, translated by Robert Hurley, M. Seem, and H. R. Lane. New York: Viking Press, 1977.

Delgado, Richard, and Jean Stefancic, eds. *Critical Race Theory: An Introduction*. New York: New York University Press, 2001.

Deloria, Philip J. *Playing Indian*. New Haven: Yale University Press, 1998.

D'Emilio, John. "Capitalism and Gay Identity." In *The Lesbian and Gay Studies Reader*, edited by Henry Abelove, Michele Aina Barale, and David M. Halperin, 467–77. New York: Routledge, 1993.

Derrida, Jacques. "Force of Law: 'Mystical Foundation of Authority.' " In *Deconstruction and the Possibility of Justice*, edited by Drucilla Cornell, Michael Rosenfeld, and David Gray Carlson, 3–67. New York: Routledge, 1992.

———. "Le Toucher: Touch/To Touch Him." *Paragraph* 16, no. 2 (1993): 122–57.

———. *Of Grammatology*. Translated by Gayatri Chakravorty Spivak. Baltimore: Johns Hopkins University Press, 1974.

———. "Racism's Last Word," translated by Peggy Kamuf. In *"Race," Writing, and Difference*, edited by Henry Louis Gates Jr., 329–38. Chicago: University of Chicago Press, 1986.

D'Souza, Dinesh. *The End of Racism: Principles for a Multiracial Society*. New York: Free Press, 1995.

duCille, Ann. *The Coupling Convention: Sex, Text, and Tradition in Black Women's Fiction*. New York: Oxford University Press, 1993.

———. "The Occult of True Black Womanhood: Critical Demeanor and Black Feminist Studies." *Signs* 19, no. 3 (spring 1994): 591–629.

———. *Skin Trade*. Cambridge: Harvard University Press, 1996.

Duggan, Lisa. *The Twilight of Equality: Neoliberalism, Cultural Politics, and the Attack on Democracy*. Boston: Beacon Press, 2003.

Echols, Alice. *Daring to Be Bad: Radical Feminism in America, 1967–1975*. Minneapolis: University of Minnesota Press, 1989.

Edelman, Lee. *No Future: Queer Theory and the Death Drive*. Durham: Duke University Press, 2004.

Elia, Nada. " 'A Man Who Wants to Be a Woman': Queerness as/and Healing Practices in Michelle Cliff's *No Telephone to Heaven*." In "Plum Nelly: New Essays in Black Queer Studies." Special issue, *Callaloo* 23, no. 1 (winter 2000): 352–65.

Eng, David, Judith Halberstam, and José Esteban Muñoz, eds. "What's Queer about Queer Studies Now?" Special issue, *Social Text* 23, nos. 3–4, 84–85 (fall–winter 2005).

Espín, Olivia M. "Cultural and Historical Influences on Sexuality in Hispanic/Latin Women: Implications for Psychotherapy." In *Pleasure and*

Danger: Exploring Female Sexuality, edited by Carole S. Vance, 149–64. Boston: Routledge, 1984.

Essed, Philomena. *Understanding Everyday Racism: An Interdisciplinary Theory*. London: Sage Publications, 1991.

Faulkner, William. *Absalom, Absalom!* New York: Library Classics of the United States, 1985 [1936].

——. *Light in August*. New York: Library Classics of the United States, 1985 [1932].

Ferguson, Roderick A. *Aberrations in Black: Toward a Queer of Color Critique*. Minneapolis: University of Minnesota Press, 2003.

Firestone, Shulamith. *The Dialectic of Sex: The Case for Feminist Revolution*. New York: Morrow, 1970.

Floyd, Kevin. *The Reification of Desire: Toward a Queer Marxism*. Minneapolis: University of Minnesota Press, 2009.

Forbes, Jack D. *Black Africans and Native Americans: Color, Race and Caste in the Evolution of Red-Black Peoples*. New York: Blackwell, 1988.

Ford, Richard Thompson. *Racial Culture: A Critique*. Princeton: Princeton University Press, 2006.

——. "What's Queer about Race?" In "After Sex? On Writing since Queer Theory." Special issue, *South Atlantic Quarterly* 106, no. 3 (summer 2007): 477–84.

Freeman, Elizabeth. "Time Binds, or, Erotohistoriography." In "What's Queer about Queer Studies Now." Special issue, *Social Text* 23: 3–4, 84–85 (fall–winter 2005): 57–68.

——. *The Wedding Complex: Forms of Belonging in Modern American Culture*. Durham: Duke University Press, 2002.

Freud, Sigmund. *The Ego and the Id*. New York: Norton, 1960.

Fuss, Diana, ed. *Human, All Too Human*. New York: Routledge, 1996.

Gerhard, Jane. *Desiring Revolution: Second-Wave Feminism and the Rewriting of American Sexual Thought, 1920–1982*. New York: Columbia University Press, 2001.

Gibson, Nigel. "Losing Sight of the Real: Recasting Merleau-Ponty in Fanon's Critique of Mannoni." In *Race and Racism in Continental Philosophy*, 129–50. Bloomington: Indiana University Press, 2003.

Gilman, Sander L. "Black Bodies, White Bodies: Toward an Iconography of Female Sexuality in Late Nineteenth-Century Art, Medicine, and Literature." In " 'Race,' Writing and Difference." Special issue, *Critical Inquiry* 12, no. 1 (autumn 1985): 223–61.

Gilroy, Paul. *Against Race: Imagining Political Culture beyond the Color Line*. Cambridge: Harvard University Press, 2000.

——. *Between Camps: Nations, Cultures and the Allure of Race*. London: Allen Lane, 2000.

Goldberg, David Theo, ed. *Anatomy of Racism*. Minneapolis: University of Minnesota Press, 1990.

——. *The Racial State*. London: Blackwell, 1993.

——. *Racist Culture: Philosophy and the Politics of Meaning*. London: Blackwell, 1993.

Goldberg, David Theo, and Philomena Essed. *Race Critical Theories: Text and Context*. London: Blackwell, 2002.

Gonzalez, G. M. James. "On 'Captive' 'Bodies,' Hidden 'Flesh' and Colonization." In *Existence in Black: An Anthology of Black Existential Philosophy*, edited by Lewis R. Gordon, 129–33. New York: Routledge, 1997.

Gooding-Williams, Robert. *Look, a Negro! Philosophical Essays on Race, Culture and Politics*. New York: Routledge, 2006.

——, ed. *Reading Rodney King, Reading Urban Uprising*. New York: Routledge, 1993.

Gordon, Avery, and Christopher Newfield. "White Philosophy." *Critical Inquiry* 20, no. 4 (summer 1994): 737–57.

Gossett, Thomas. *Race: The History of an Idea in America*. New York: Oxford University Press, 1997.

Grosz, Elizabeth. "Merleau-Ponty and Irigaray in the Flesh." In *Merleau-Ponty: Interiority and Exteriority, Psychic Life and the World*, edited by Dorothea Olkowski and James Morley, 145–66. Albany: State University of New York Press, 1999.

——. *The Nick of Time: Politics, Evolution, and the Untimely*. Durham: Duke University Press, 2004.

——. *Space, Time and Perversion: Essays on the Politics of Bodies*. New York: Routledge, 1995.

Halberstam, Judith. *In a Queer Time and Place: Transgender Bodies, Subcultural Lives*. Durham: Duke University Press, 2005.

——. "Shame and White Gay Masculinity." *Social Text* 23, nos. 3–4, 84–85 (fall–winter 2005): 219–33.

Hall, Stuart. "What's the 'Black' in Black Popular Culture?" In *Stuart Hall: Critical Dialogues in Cultural Studies*, edited by David Morley and Kuan-Hsing Chen, 465–75. London: Routledge, 1996.

Halle, Randall. *Queer Social Philosophy: Critical Readings from Kant to Adorno*. Urbana: University of Illinois Press, 2004.

Halley, Janet. " 'Like Race' Arguments." In *What's Left of Theory? New Work on the Politics of Literary Theory*, edited by Judith Butler, John Guillory, and Kendall Thomas, 40–74. New York: Routledge, 2000.

——. *Split Decisions: How and Why to Take a Break from Feminism*. Princeton: Princeton University Press, 2006.

Halperin, David. "Is There a History of Sexuality?" *History and Theory* 28, no. 3 (October 1989): 257–74.

Hames-García, Michael P. "Can Queer Theory Be Critical Theory?" In *New Critical Theory: Essays on Liberation*, edited by William S. Wilkerson and Jeffrey Paris, 201–22. Lanham, Md.: Rowman and Littlefield, 2001.

Hammonds, Evelynn. "Black (W)holes and the Geometry of Black Female Sexuality." In "More Gender Trouble: Feminism Meets Queer Theory." Special issue, *differences* 6, nos. 2–3 (summer–fall 1994): 126–45.

Haraway, Donna. *Modest_Witness@Second_Millenium.FemaleMan©_Meets_ OncoMouse*. New York: Routledge, 1997.

Hardt, Michael, and Antonio Negri. *Empire*. Cambridge: Harvard University Press, 2000.

Harkins, Gillian. *Everybody's Family Romance: Reading Incest in Neoliberal America*. Minneapolis: University of Minnesota Press, 2010.

Harper, Philip Brian. "The Evidence of Felt Intuition: Minority Experience, Everyday Life, and Critical Speculative Knowledge." In *Black Queer Studies: A Critical Anthology*, edited by E. Patrick Johnson and Mae G. Henderson, 106–23. Durham: Duke University Press, 2005.

——. *Private Affairs: Critical Ventures in the Culture of Social Relations*. New York: New York University Press, 1999.

——. " 'Take Me Home': Location, Identity, Transnational Exchange." In "Plum Nelly: New Essays in Black Queer Studies." Special issue, *Callaloo* 23, no. 1 (winter 2000): 461–78.

Harper, Philip Brian, Anne McClintock, Jose Esteban Munoz, and Trish Rosen, eds. "Queer Transexions of Race, Nation and Gender." Special issue, *Social Text* 15, nos. 3–4, 52–53 (fall–winter 1997).

Harris, Cheryl I. "Whiteness as Property." *Harvard Law Review* 106, no. 8 (June 1993): 1707–91.

Harris, Laura Alexandra. "Queer Black Feminism: The Pleasure Principle." *Feminist Review* 54 (autumn 1996): 3–30.

Hart, Lynda. *Between the Body and the Flesh: Performing Sadomasochism*. New York: Columbia University Press, 1998.

——. *Fatal Women*. Princeton: Princeton University Press, 1994.

Hartman, Saidiya V. *Scenes of Subjection: Terror, Slavery, and Self-Making in Nineteenth-Century America*. New York: Oxford University Press, 1997.

Hayles, N. Katherine. *How We Became Posthuman: Virtual Bodies in Cybernetics, Literature, and Informatics*. Chicago: University of Chicago Press, 1999.

Heinämaa, Sara. *Toward a Phenomenology of Sexual Difference: Husserl, Merleau-Ponty, Beauvoir*. Lanham, Md.: Rowman and Littlefield, 2003.

Henderson, Mae G. "James Baldwin: Expatriation, Homosexual Panic, and Man's

Estate." In "Plum Nelly: New Essays in Black Queer Studies." Special issue, *Callaloo* 23, no. 1 (winter 2000): 313–27.

Hennessey, Rosemary. *Profit and Pleasure: Sexual Identities in Late Capitalism.* New York: Routledge, 2000.

Henry, Paget. "African and Afro-Caribbean Existential Philosophies." In *Existence in Black: An Anthology of Black Existential Philosophy*, edited by Lewis R. Gordon, 13–36. New York: Routledge, 1997.

Holland, Sharon P. "The Beached Whale." GLQ 17, no. 1 (2001): 89–95.

——. *Raising the Dead: Readings of Death and (Black) Subjectivity.* Durham: Duke University Press, 2000.

——. "To Touch the Mother's C[o]untry: Siting Audre Lorde's Erotics." In *Lesbian Erotics*, edited by Karla Jay, 212–26. New York: New York University Press, 1995.

Howe, Irving. *William Faulkner: A Critical Study.* Chicago: University of Chicago Press, 1975.

Huffer, Lynne. *Mad for Foucault: Rethinking the Foundations of Queer Theory.* New York: Columbia University Press, 2010.

Hull, Gloria T., Patricia Bell Scott, and Barbara Smith, eds. *All the Women Are White, All the Blacks Are Men, but Some of Us Are Brave: Black Women's Studies.* Old Westbury, N.Y.: Feminist Press, 1982.

Jefferson, Thomas. *Notes on the State of Virginia*, edited by Frank Shuffelton. New York: Penguin, 1999 [1785].

Johnson, E. Patrick. " 'Quare' Studies, or (Almost) Everything I Know about Queer Studies I Learned from My Grandmother." In *Black Queer Studies: A Critical Anthology*, edited by E. Patrick Johnson and Mae G. Henderson, 124–57. Durham: Duke University Press.

Johnson, E. Patrick, and Mae G. Henderson, eds. *Black Queer Studies: A Critical Anthology.* Durham: Duke University Press, 2005.

Justice, Daniel Heath, Mark Rifkin, and Bethany Schneider. "Sexuality, Nationality, Indigeneity." Special issue, GLQ 16, nos. 1–2 (2010).

King, Jason. "Any Love: Silence, Theft, and Rumor in the Work of Luther Vandross." In "Plum Nelly: New Essays in Black Queer Studies." Special issue, *Callaloo* 23, no. 1 (winter 2000): 422–47.

Kruks, Sonia. "Beauvoir's Time/Our Time: The Renaissance in Simone de Beauvoir Studies." *Feminist Studies* 31, no. 2 (summer 2005): 286–309.

Lee, Joon Oluchi. "The Joy of the Castrated Boy." *Social Text* 23, nos. 3–4, 84–85 (fall–winter 2005): 35–56.

Levinas, Emmanuel. *Emmanuel Levinas: Basic Philosophical Writings*, edited by Adriaan Theodoor Peperzak, Simon Critchley, and Robert Bernasconi. Bloomington: Indiana University Press, 1996.

——. *Time and the Other*, translated by Richard A. Cohen. Pittsburgh: Duquesne University Press, 1987.

Linden, Robin Ruth, Darlene R. Pagano, Diana E. H. Russell, and Susan Leigh Star, eds. *Against Sadomasochism: A Radical Feminist Analysis*. East Palo Alto, Calif.: Frog in the Well, 1982.

Lippet, Akira Mizuta. *Electric Animal: Toward a Rhetoric of Wildlife*. Minneapolis: University of Minnesota Press, 2000.

Lorde, Audre. "Interview with Audre Lorde." In *Against Sadomasochism: A Radical Feminist Analysis*, edited by Robin Ruth Linden et al., 68–71. East Palo Alto, Calif.: Frog in the Well, 1982.

——. "Uses of the Erotic: The Erotic as Power." In *Sister Outsider*, 53–59. Trumansburg, N.Y.: Crossing Press, 1984.

Lubiano, Wahneema, ed. *The House That Race Built: Black Americans, U.S. Terrain*. New York: Pantheon Books, 1997.

Martin, Biddy. "Sexualities without Genders and Other Queer Utopias." *Diacritics* 24, nos. 2–3 (1994): 104–21.

Mayberry, Marlalee, Banu Subramanim, and Lisa H. Weasel, eds. *Feminist Science: A New Generation*. New York: Routledge, 2001.

McBride, Dwight A. "Introduction: 'How Much Time Do You Want for Your Progress?' New Approaches to James Baldwin." In *James Baldwin Now*, edited by Dwight A. McBride, 1–9. New York: New York University Press, 1999.

——. *Why I Hate Abercrombie & Fitch: Essays on Race and Sexuality*. New York: New York University Press, 2005.

McCall, Leslie. "The Complexity of Intersectionality." *Signs* 30 (2005): 1771–800.

McClintock, Anne, and Rob Nixon. "No Names Apart: The Separation of Word and History in Derrida's 'Le Dernier Mot du Racisme.'" In *"Race," Writing and Difference*, edited by Henry Louis Gates Jr., 339–53. Chicago: University of Chicago Press, 1985.

Merleau-Ponty, Maurice. *The Phenomenology of Perception*. New York: Routledge, 2002.

Michaels, Walter Benn. "The No Drop Rule." *Critical Inquiry* 20, no. 4 (summer 1994): 758–69.

——. *Our America: Nativism, Modernism, Pluralism*. Durham: Duke University Press, 1997.

——. "Race into Culture: A Critical Genealogy of Cultural Identity." *Critical Inquiry* 18, no. 4 (summer 1992): 655–85.

Miles, Robert. *Racism after "Race Relations."* London: Routledge, 1993.

Miles, Robert, and Malcom Brown. *Racism*. 2nd ed. London: Routledge, 2003.

Miles, Tiya, and Sharon Holland, eds. *Crossing Waters, Crossing Worlds: The African Diaspora in Indian Country*. Durham: Duke University Press, 2005.

Mills, Charles. *Blackness Visible: Essays on Philosophy and Race*. Ithaca: Cornell University Press, 1998.

——. *The Racial Contract*. Ithaca: Cornell University Press, 1997.

Mohanty, Satya. *Literary Theory and the Claims of History: Postmodernism, Objectivity, Multicultural Politics*. Ithaca: Cornell University Press, 1997.

Moi, Toril. *Simone de Beauvoir: The Making of an Intellectual Woman*. Cambridge: Blackwell, 1994.

——. "While We Wait: The English Translation of *The Second Sex*." *Signs* 27, no. 4 (summer 2002): 1005–35.

Moraga, Cherríe. *Loving in the War Years: Lo que nunca pasó por sus labios*. Boston: South End Press, 1983.

Moran, Rachel. *Interracial Dating: The Regulation of Race and Romance*. Chicago: University of Chicago Press, 2001.

Morgan, Robin. "The Politics of Sado-Masochistic Fantasies." In *Against Sadomasochism: A Radical Feminist Analysis*, edited by Robin Ruth Linden et al., 109–23. East Palo Alto, Calif.: Frog in the Well, 1982.

——. *Sisterhood Is Powerful: An Anthology of Writings from the Women's Liberation Movement*. New York: Random House, 1970.

Morrison, Toni. *Beloved*. New York: Alfred A. Knopf, 1987.

——. "Home." In *The House That Race Built: Black Americans, U.S. Terrain*, edited by Wahneema Lubiano, 3–12. New York: Pantheon, 1997.

——. *Playing in the Dark*. Cambridge: Harvard University Press, 1992.

Morton, Donald. "Birth of the Cyberqueer." *PMLA* 110, no. 3 (May 1995): 369–81.

Moten, Fred. "The Case for Blackness." *Criticism* 50, no. 2 (spring 2008): 177–218.

——. *In the Break: The Aesthetics of the Black Radical Tradition*. Minneapolis: University of Minnesota Press, 2003.

Moya, Paula. *Learning from Experience: Minority Identities, Multicultural Struggles*. Berkeley: University of California Press, 2002.

Mullen, Harryette. *Muse and Drudge*. Berkeley: University of California Press, 2002.

——. *Sleeping with the Dictionary*. Berkeley: University of California Press, 2002.

——. *S*PeRMK*T*. Philadelphia: Singing Horse, 1995.

——. *Tree Tall Woman: Poems*. Galveston, Tex.: Energy Earth Communications, 1981.

Muñoz, José Esteban. *Cruising Utopia: The Then and There of Queer Futurity*. New York: New York University Press, 2009.

——. *Disidentifications: Queers of Color and the Performance of Politics*. Minneapolis: University of Minnesota Press, 1999.

Nash, Jennifer. "Re-Thinking Intersectionality." *Feminist Review* 89, no. 1 (2008): 1–15.

———. "Strange Bedfellows: Black Feminism and Antipornography Feminism." *Social Text* 26, no. 4 (winter 2008): 51–76.

Nelkin, Dorothy, and Susan Lindee. "The Media-ted Gene: Stories of Gender and Race." In *Deviant Bodies: Critical Perspectives on Difference in Science and Popular Culture*, edited by Jennifer Terry and Jacqueline Urla, 387–402. Bloomington: Indiana University Press, 1995.

Norman, Brian. " 'We' in Redux: The Combahee River Collective's *Black Feminist Statement*." *differences* 18, no. 2 (2007): 103–32.

Nyong'o, Tavia. "Punk'd Theory." *Social Text* 23, nos. 3–4, 84–85 (fall–winter 2005): 19–34.

O'Grady, Lorraine. "Nefertiti/Devonia Evangeline." *Art Journal* 56, no. 4 (winter 1997): 64–65.

———. "Olympia's Maid: Reclaiming Black Female Subjectivity." In *New Feminist Criticism: Art, Identity, Action*, edited by Joanna Frueh, Cassandra Langer, and Arlene Raven, 152–70. New York: Harper Collins, 1994.

Omi, Michael, and Howard Winant. *Racial Formation in the United States: From the 1960s to the 1990s*. 2nd ed. New York: Routledge, 1994.

Outlaw, Lucius. "Toward a Critical Theory of 'Race.' " In *Anatomy of Racism*, edited by David Theo Goldberg, 58–82. Minneapolis: University of Minnesota Press, 1990.

Pateman, Carole. *The Sexual Contract*. Stanford: Stanford University Press, 1988.

Pateman, Carole, and Charles Mills. *Contract and Domination*. Cambridge: Polity Press, 2007.

Perez, Hiram. "You Can Have My Brown Body and Eat It, Too!" *Social Text* 23, nos. 3–4, 84–85 (fall–winter 2005): 171–91.

Piper, Adrian. "Passing for White, Passing for Black." In *Passing and the Fictions of Identity*, edited by Elaine K. Ginsberg, 234–69. Durham: Duke University Press, 1996.

Preston, William A. "Nietzsche on Blacks." In *Existence in Black: An Anthology of Black Existential Philosophy*, edited by Lewis R. Gordon, 167–72. New York: Routledge, 1997.

Prosser, Jay. *Second Skins: The Body Narratives of Transsexuality*. New York: Columbia University Press, 1998.

Puar, Jasbir. *Terrorist Assemblages: Homonationalism in Queer Times*. Durham: Duke University Press, 2007.

Reid-Pharr, Robert. *Conjugal Union: The Body, the House, and the Black American*. New York: Oxford University Press, 1999.

———. *Once You Go Black: Choice, Desire, and the Black American Intellectual*. New York: New York University Press, 2007.

Rich, Adrienne. "Compulsory Heterosexuality and Lesbian Existence." In *Powers of Desire: The Politics of Sexuality*, edited by Ann Snitow, Christine Stansell, and Sharon Thompson, 177–205. New York: Monthly Review Press, 1983.

Richeson, Jennifer A., and Nicole Shelton. "Negotiating Interracial Interactions: Costs, Consequences and Possibilities." *Current Directions in Psychological Science* 16, no. 6 (2007): 316–20.

Roediger, David. "White Workers, New Democrats, and Affirmative Action." In *Colored White: Transcending the Racial Past*, 55–67. Berkeley: University of California Press, 2002.

Rose, Jacqueline, and Juliet Mitchell, eds. *Feminine Sexuality: Jacques Lacan and the École Freudienne*. New York: Norton, 1982.

Ross, Marlon B. "Beyond the Closet as a Raceless Paradigm." In *Black Queer Studies: A Critical Anthology*, edited by E. Patrick Johnson and Mae G. Henderson, 161–89. Durham: Duke University Press, 2005.

——. "Camping the Dirty Dozens: The Queer Resources of Black Nationalist Invective." In "Plum Nelly: New Essays in Black Queer Studies." Special issue, *Callaloo* 23, no. 1 (winter 2000): 290–312.

——. "White Fantasies of Desire: Baldwin and the Racial Identities of Sexuality." In *James Baldwin Now*, edited by Dwight A. McBride, 13–55. New York: New York University Press, 1999.

Rubin, Gayle. "Thinking Sex: Notes for a Radical Theory of the Politics of Sexuality." In *Pleasure and Danger: Exploring Female Sexuality*, edited by Carole S. Vance, 267–319. Boston: Routledge, 1984.

Scott, Jacqueline. "The Price of the Ticket: A Genealogy and Revaluation of Race." In *Critical Affinities: Nietzsche and African American Thought*, edited by Jacqueline Scott and A. Todd Franklin, 149–71. New York: State University of New York Press, 2006.

Sedgwick, Eve Kosofsky. *Epistemology of the Closet*. Berkeley: University of California Press, 1990.

Sikka, Sonia. "Heidegger and Race." In *Race and Racism in Continental Philosophy*, edited by Robert Bernasconi with Sybol Cook, 74–97. Bloomington: Indiana University Press, 2003.

Silva, Denise Ferreira da. *Toward a Global Idea of Race*. Minneapolis: University of Minnesota Press, 2007.

Simons, Margaret A. *Beauvoir and "The Second Sex": Feminism, Race and the Origins of Existentialism*. Lanham, Md.: Rowman and Littlefield, 1999.

——. "The Silencing of Simone de Beauvoir: Guess What's Missing from *The Second Sex*." *Women's Studies International Forum* 6, no. 5 (1983): 559–64.

Snead, James A. "Repetition as a Figure of Black Culture." In *Out There: Marginalization and Contemporary Cultures*, edited by Russell Ferguson, Martha Gever, Trinh T. Minh-ha, and Cornel West, 213–30. Cambridge: MIT Press, 1990.

Somerville, Siobhan B. *Queering the Color Line: Race and the Invention of Homosexuality in American Culture*. Durham: Duke University Press, 2000.

———. "Scientific Racism and the Emergence of the Homosexual Body." *Journal of the History of Sexuality* 5, no. 2 (1994): 243–66.

Spillers, Hortense J. *Black, White, and in Color: Essays on American Literature and Culture*. Chicago: University of Chicago Press, 2003.

———. "Interstices: A New Drama of Words." In *Pleasure and Danger: Exploring Female Sexuality*, edited by Carole S. Vance, 73–100. Boston: Routledge, 1984.

———. "Mama's Baby, Papa's Maybe: An American Grammar Book." In *Black, White, and in Color: Essays on American Literature and Culture*, 203–29. Chicago: University of Chicago Press, 2003.

Spivak, Gayatri Chakravorty. "Race before Racism: The Disappearance of the American." *boundary 2* 25, no. 2 (summer 1998): 35–53.

Springer, Kimberly. *Living for the Revolution: Black Feminist Organizations, 1968–1980*. Durham: Duke University Press, 2005.

Stockton, Kathryn Bond. "Growing Sideways, or Versions of the Queer Child: The Ghost, the Homosexual, the Freudian, the Innocent, and the Interval of Animal." In *Curiouser: On the Queerness of Children*, edited by Steven Bruhm and Natasha Hurley, 277–315. Minneapolis: University of Minnesota Press, 2004.

Stone, Betsey. *Sisterhood Is Powerful*. New York: Pathfinder Press, 1970.

Sundstrom, Ronald R. "Douglass and Du Bois' Der Schwarze Volksgeist." In *Race and Racism in Continental Philosophy*, edited by Robert Bernasconi with Sybol Cook, 32–52. Bloomington: Indiana University Press, 2003.

Traister, Bryce. "The Object of Study; or, Are We Being Transnational Yet?" *Journal of Transnational American Studies* 2, no. 1 (2010): 1–28.

Tyler, Carole-Anne. *Female Impersonation*. New York: Routledge, 2003.

———. "Passing: Narcissism, Identity and Difference." In *differences* 6, nos. 2–3 (1994): 212–48.

Vance, Carole S., ed. *Pleasure and Danger: Exploring Female Sexuality*. Boston: Routledge, 1984.

Vasseleu, Carolyn. *Textures of Light: Vision and Touch in Irigaray, Levinas and Merleau-Ponty*. New York: Routledge, 1998.

Walcott, Rinaldo. "Outside in Black Studies: Reading from a Queer Place in the Diaspora." In *Black Queer Studies: A Critical Anthology*, edited by E. Patrick Johnson and Mae G. Henderson, 90–105. Durham: Duke University Press, 2005.

Wald, Priscilla. *Contagious: Cultures, Carriers, and the Outbreak Narrative*. Durham: Duke University Press, 2008.

Walker, Alice. "A Letter of the Times, or Should This Sado-Masochism Be Saved?" In *Against Sadomasochism: A Radical Feminist Analysis*, edited by Robin Ruth Linden et al., 205–8. East Palo Alto, Calif.: Frog in the Well, 1982.

Warner, Michael. *The Trouble with Normal: Sex, Politics and the Ethics of Queer Life*. Cambridge: Harvard University Press, 1999.

Weed, Elizabeth. "The More Things Change." *differences* 6, nos. 2–3 (summer–fall 1994): 249–73.

Wiegman, Robyn. *American Anatomies: Theorizing Race and Gender*. Durham: Duke University Press, 1995.

Wilson, Judith. *Lorraine O'Grady: Photomontages*. New York: INTAR Gallery, 1991.

Wilson, William Julius. *The Declining Significance of Race: Blacks and Changing American Institutions*. Chicago: University of Chicago Press, 1978.

Winchester, James. "Nietzsche's Racial Profiling." In *Race and Racism in Modern Philosophy*, edited by Andrew Valls, 255–76. Ithaca: Cornell University Press, 2005.

Wing, Adrien Katherine, ed. *Global Critical Race Feminism: An International Reader*. New York: New York University Press, 2000.

Womack, Craig. *Red on Red: Native American Literary Separatism*. Minneapolis: University of Minnesota Press, 1999.

Wright, Michelle Maria. *Becoming Black: Creating Identity in the African Diaspora*. Durham: Duke University Press, 2004.

Index

apartheid, Derrida on language of, 98
Appiah, Kwame Anthony, 41–42, 117n8, 122n10, 129n52
Asante, Molefi Kete, 141n18
autonomy, erotic and role of, 46–47, 129n4

Baldwin, James, 10, 71, 75
Barrett, Lindon, 17
Baxandall, Rosalyn, 124n19
Beauvoir, Simone de, 9, 146n23; on erotic, 46–48, 51–52, 59–60, 131n19; on masculinity, 91, 130n10; on slavery, 52–53; translations of, 131n16
Bell, Derrick, 26
Beloved (Morrison), 96–98
Bereano, Nancy, 133n21
Bergoffen, Deborah, 1, 132n17
Berlant, Lauren, 105
Bernasconi, Robert, 127n46
beyond: critical race theory and concept of, 17–39; Gilroy's formula for, 26–27
"Beyond the Closet as Raceless Paradigm" (Ross), 74–75, 139n52
biological, queer theory and, 59–64
black body images: black feminism and, 52–57; black intellectual movement and, 118n10; black queer theory and, 68, 70, 140n14; erotic and racism in, 45–46; historicism of, 20–21; racism and, 4–5; slavery and, 32–39
"Black (W)holes and the Geometry of Black Female Sexuality" (Hammonds), 68–69
black feminist theory: black body images and, 51–52; critical race theory and, 22–34; erotic and, 54–57; queer theory and, 124n19, 135n33; sexuality, belonging, citizenship, and race in, 143n34; subjectivity and pleasure and, 120n18
black intellectual movement: Afrocentricity and, 141n18; black body imagery and, 118n10; black queer theory and, 71–72, 86–93

black nationalism, black queer studies and, 70
black queer studies: African American studies and, 73–74; black body images and, 70; intersectionality in, 79–85; queer of color critique and, 66–93, 140n10; queer theory and, 66–93
Black Queer Studies (Johnson and Henderson), 73–76, 81–82
Black Queer Studies: A Critical Anthology (Brody and McBride), 69–70, 142n26
black/white binary: Bonilla-Silva's discussion of, 30–32; categorization of, 118n15; critical race theory and, 28–29; desire and racism and, 43–64; queer theory and, 58–64; racism and, 9–11
"blood strangers" concept, racism and, 6–7
Bodies That Matter (Butler), 71, 139n5
"Bollywood Spectacles" (Gopinath), 85–86
Bonilla-Silva, Eduardo, 19–20, 30–34
Borderlands/La Frontera (Anzaldúa), 71–72
borderland theory, black queer theory and, 72–93
Braidotti, Rosi, 67–68
British cultural studies: critical race theory and, 25, 28; queer theory and, 83
Brody, DeVere, 69–70
Brown, Malcolm, 4, 24–25, 28–30, 32
Brown, Wendy, 65–66
Bryant, Roy, 3, 116n2
Butler, Judith, 134n23, 134n26, 138n48; black feminist theory and, 23; black queer studies and, 42; black queer theory and, 71; on Eurocentrism in feminist theory, 67–68; Hammond's critique of, 139n5; race and the erotic and, 45, 51, 53–57, 62–64
Byrd, James, 3

Califia, Pat, 55
Callaloo (journal), 69, 76

SHARON PATRICIA HOLLAND is associate professor of English, African
and African American studies, and women's studies at Duke University.

Library of Congress Cataloging-in-Publication Data
Holland, Sharon Patricia.
The erotic life of racism / Sharon Patricia Holland.
p. cm.
Includes bibliographical references and index.
ISBN 978-0-8223-5195-5 (cloth : alk. paper)
ISBN 978-0-8223-5206-8 (pbk. : alk. paper)
1. Racism—United States. 2. Prejudices—United States.
3. United States—Race relations. I. Title.
HM1091.H65 2012
305.8—dc23
2011035973

P O C K E ~~T~~ ~~HEALERS~~

Vitamin B

VITAMINS BALANCING BODY & MIND

Stephanie Pedersen

A DORLING KINDERSLEY BOOK

CONTENTS